An Obesity of Grief

"Lynn Haraldson's *An Obesity of Grief* is a deeply moving, emotional and honest memoir—a story of survival. After losing her young husband in a horrific train accident, leaving her with their weeks-old newborn, Lynn was almost consumed by her grief. In the years that followed, she overcame trauma, faced anxiety and depression head-on, developed a healthy relationship with food and her body, and ultimately found peace and happiness. Lynn's courage and strength are inspirational, and her story illustrates that even through unimaginable pain, you can still find beauty and purpose."

—**Joy Bauer**, MS, RDN, CDN,
Nutrition Expert for NBC's *Today Show*

"After the death of her husband, a question circles and coils within author Lynn Haraldson for more than two decades: how did he not hear the train? It is a question that twists and constricts, creating heavy layers of complex grief enough to weigh down a life. But *An Obesity of Grief* is a radiant release. Here, the search for a long-lost answer leads her to the intersection where her young husband died and to a deeper understanding than she could have ever imagined—one that allows her to forgive him for dying and forgive herself for doubt. I will love you, again, says the poem by Ellen Bass from which the author borrowed her luminous memoir's title. This is a story that anyone who has known long-term grief will hold tight to their heart. It is a story of learning to love ourselves in grief. And it is the story of how love lost too soon can still grow old alongside us, even as we move on."

—**Diane Zinna**, Author of *The All-Night Sun*
and *Letting Grief Speak: Writing Portals for Life After Loss*

"Lynn Haraldson doesn't pull any punches on the realities of grief and trauma in this fast-paced, insightful memoir. After losing her young husband when she was just nineteen years old—with an eleven-day-old baby at home—Haraldson begins the long and painful process of figuring out how to live a life she never envisioned for herself. It's not until she eventually learns how to acknowledge her grief that she begins to move forward, address her anger, and tackle health challenges caused by excess weight. Her account of helping her then-teenage daughter come to know her deceased father, many years after he died, is especially poignant, and offers hope to widowed parents that it's never too late to support our kids through their losses, even as we deal with our own."

—**Jenny Lisk,** Author of *Future Widow,*
Host of the *Widowed Parent Podcast*

"After an unimaginable loss at nineteen, Lynn Haraldson captures the all-encompassing nature of loss and love over a lifetime in her beautiful memoir. I found myself alternatively weeping and cheering as Lynn unravels the layers of her grief with unflinching honesty, poignant detail, and growing self-compassion. Her boundless courage and willingness to embrace the messiness of grief is a hopeful and triumphant tale."

—**Shauna Reid**, Author of *The Amazing Adventures of Dietgirl*

"As a fan of Haraldson's earlier book, *Common Ground*, and someone who has followed her work and writing, I was excited to get a sneak preview of her book Obesity of Grief. In the plethora of 'grief' books, it stands out in its spotlight on the unusual and unexpected ways that unresolved grief can show up in our behaviors, our addictions, and other aspects of both our emotional and physical health. From her own experience, Haraldson dispels the myth that the grieving process is in any way linear or typical, and she bravely pushes back on our society's pressure to 'just get over it.' She inspired me with her hard-won lessons about herself, about grief, and about love. Grief counselors will find this book to be a healing companion for their patients, regardless of where they are in their grief journey."

—**Elizabeth H. Cottrel**l, Author of *Heartspoken: How to Write Notes that Connect, Comfort, Encourage, and Inspire*

"Lynn's Haraldson's heart-wrenching story is one that so many of us fear: losing our spouse after just having a newborn baby. In her memoir, *An Obesity of Grief*, Lynn details her struggle in learning to support a new life that's just beginning while also grieving a life that ended tragically and abruptly. Her journey reminds us how precious life is, and how, at any moment, our world can be shattered. The hardships and trials that Lynn faced as a result of her grief are undeniable, and yet her ability to overcome, find her strength, and rise once again is an inspiration for all of us. She is a force and a guide for all of us who are slowly making our way through grief and loss."

—**Nesreen Ahmed**, MS, PCC, CPQC, Founder and CEO
of Harbor Light Coaching, LLC

"Lynn Haraldson's memoir, *An Obesity of Grief*, is a guide to navigating grief and the trauma that often accompanies it. Her book is approachable and easily relatable for anyone on their own passage to healing. Through a compelling story, she provides an honest and heartfelt look into her own grieving process and how a traumatic loss in early adulthood impacted her ability to cope and move on with her life. Not only can her story validate the experiences of those who suffer loss and trauma, but she also shares her method of overcoming and healing. She chronicles in detail her experiences (both positive and negative) with medication; practicing mindfulness, including meditation; seeing various mental health practitioners; and ultimately, what works to help her get to a place of acceptance and healing. As a yoga teacher and mental health therapist, I am in love with this inspiring journey Lynn goes through!"

—**Allison Steinwand**, MS, LPC, QMHP, PMH-C, RYT-500,
Archway Counseling & Wellness LLC

"We cling to our grief because it keeps our loved ones alive and because we want to understand what has happened, and why. Growing up in the Midwest where stoicism is often the response to tragedy, Lynn Haraldson discovers that understanding traumatic grief is the slow peeling of an onion because there are many layers of emotion underneath. She also learns that being kind to yourself when grieving is important, and that while our grief will never go away, we can reach a place where we feel joy and sadness at the same time."

—**Mark Liebenow**, Grief Explorer and Author of *Mountains of Life*

"Lynn Haraldson's memoir, *An Obesity of Grief: A Journey from Traumatic Loss to Undying Love*, is a testament to how our connections to those we love don't end with death. With honesty and courage, she lays out her journey from nineteen-year-old new mother and widow, deep in grief and struggling to find her place in the world after the tragic death of her husband, to the mother of two adult daughters, who finally understands that we can indeed hold both love and grief and that embracing our lives does not erase the person we lost. Haraldson's clear prose allows us an intimate portrait of deep sadness and moments of illumination. *An Obesity of Grief* is a must-read for anyone navigating early loss and those who support them."

—**Casey Mulligan Walsh**, Grief Essayist and Author of *Still, Best of the Net Nominee*

An Obesity of Grief

of

Grief

A Journey From Traumatic Loss
to Undying Love

LYNN HARALDSON

VIRGINIA BEACH
CAPE CHARLES

An Obesity of Grief

by Lynn Haraldson

Published by

köehlerbooks™

3705 Shore Drive
Virginia Beach, VA 23455
800-435-4811
www.koehlerbooks.com

For every grieving person who's been told,
"You'll get over it."

Table of Contents

Author's Note

I have a fairly good memory, but it's my penchant for hanging on to old journals and letters that helped create this book. I relied on them to relay the events and conversations presented here, and I wrote with utmost attention to the truth as I experienced it. A few names have been changed or omitted to support privacy.

The title of this book is a line from the Ellen Bass poem *The Thing Is*. She has graciously given her blessing for me to use it.

Part One

Life After Death

CHAPTER 1

March 1983

My husband is dead. At least that's what they tell me. They won't let me see him, so I can't say for sure. It's been three days, but I still expect him to walk in and apologize for being late. That would be more like him, being late rather than dead. Late I can forgive. I don't know what to do with dead.

They say he was on his way home from the grain elevator when a train hit his tractor. I remember hearing a train that morning, blowing its whistle longer than usual, like it was trying to draw someone's attention. I'd looked out the window and had seen a train stopped on the tracks a half mile away, but the pig shed blocked my view of the intersection.

How could I have known I had audibly witnessed my husband's death? Bruce told me he'd be working in the machine shed all morning, and as far as I knew, that's where he was. I'd gone back to folding diapers.

Except for the moments I nurse Carlene in our bedroom—and even then, I don't get much privacy—the bathroom is my refuge, the only place people leave me alone, and I can think without interruption. Today is the funeral, so I linger in the shower, crying where no one can hear me.

I am riddled with hemorrhoids, my breasts leak like sieves, and I am tired. Bone weary tired. I still struggle with nursing due to a plugged milk duct, but for the few days that we were a family of three, I hadn't struggled alone. Bruce rocked and sang to Carlene while I slept, and in the middle of the night, he got up with me, and we watched *Rocky and Bullwinkle* to distract me from the soreness. We were finding our rhythm, but now, our burgeoning rhythm is gone, lost in the chaos of death. As friends, family, and a few people I don't know, at least not well, bring their tears and casseroles to our farm, Carlene and I are eyed-up and clung to by people in search of comfort. But how am I to soothe the pain of others when I don't know what to do with my own? I especially don't know what to do with the questions: Could his nephew have Bruce's archery set? (*I didn't know Bruce had an archery set.*) Do you think you'll get married again? (*Wait . . . aren't I still married?*) Maybe we should adopt the baby? After all, you're only nineteen . . .

Our pediatrician called yesterday. He'd heard about the accident on the news.

"How are you?" he asked.

"I'm okay," I said, even though I can't eat.

Gently, like he was talking to a child, he suggested I supplement nursing with formula.

"That wasn't part of our plan."

"Lynn, that was before. You need to take care of yourself, and you need to take care of Carlene."

I turn off the water and wrap myself in Bruce's ratty brown terry bathrobe and sit cross-legged on the vanity, facing the mirror, like I did when we got ready for a date or for church. Bruce would shave, shirtless, while I put on my makeup.

I think about Bruce's smooth skin, firm stomach, and the soft brown chest hair that trails in a narrow line to his belly button, and I wonder again what is in the casket that I'm not allowed to see. Will his body be dressed in the outfit I picked out: a dark-blue jacket, gray slacks, and a cream knit tie? Or will everything be neatly folded next to an assortment of remains?

His mother insisted he be buried with the onyx ring she'd given him when he graduated from college. I reluctantly gave that up, but I insisted on keeping his wedding band. That and his wallet were all I got back from the accident. Not his coveralls or boots or the kerchief he kept in his back pocket. Not even the jar of Carmex from his coat. His tractor disappeared, too. They said it was taken somewhere I'd never have to see it, just like his body.

I rub foundation on my face, trying to cover the dark circles under my eyes, and I imagine Bruce standing next to me, knotting his tie, something he tried many times to teach me.

"Place this end over that end," he'd say, guiding my hands with his. "Now loop this end under the other end. Yeah, yeah, just like that, and up through the top—" And soon my hands would be on my lap while he completed the knot.

He'd laugh and say, "Someday."

I turn on the radio. Toto's "I Won't Hold You Back" is playing. We loved this song in a "we'll never break up" kind of way.

How foolish we were to think we'd be together forever.

"We were supposed to be married for seventy-five years," I want to say to him. "We talked about this, on the couch that Sunday when your parents were in Iowa, and we had the house to ourselves. You showed me that card in your wallet, the one with the alphabet in sign language on one side and Kama Sutra positions on the other. We practiced with our clothes on and laughed so hard we cried. Then we went to your bedroom and . . ."

I turn off the radio and climb off the vanity. It's time to get dressed.

Our closet is in the bathroom, an addition Bruce's parents built years ago because the only bathroom in the house was upstairs. I open the door to my side and take out the one outfit that fits other than maternity clothes—a stretchy white knit skirt with an elastic waistband and a short white jacket with three-quarter length sleeves that I bought in anticipation of the baby's baptism.

"What color shirt should I wear underneath?" I'd asked Bruce as I paged through the JC Penney's catalog.

"Purple," he said. "It's springy."

Spring was his favorite season. Or was it fall? He loved so

many things that I don't remember. Of the two of us, he was more optimistic. Even his blood type was B positive while mine is O negative. Bruce was always on the side of the underdog, the suffering cow, the runt of the litter.

A month ago, when our sows were farrowing, Bruce spent several hours each night in the pig shed. I'd never seen a pig, or anything, be born, so when one of the sows was about to give birth, he came to the house and woke me up.

I smelled him before I saw his shadow outlined in the dark, a combination of cold air, hay, and manure. He was on his haunches, touching my hair.

"Lynn," he whispered. "The pigs are coming. Do you want to watch?"

I got dressed and put on the parka that I could no longer zip over my belly. It was biting cold, but the stars shone bright as we walked across the yard. He'd tucked his arm in mine to keep me from falling. Our breath, frosted like a cloud, lingered in the air before evaporating. The only sound was our boots crunching snow.

A heat lamp hovered over the sow, who was lying on her nest of straw. One piglet was already born and nursing when another one plopped out onto the straw. He laid there, stunned, with thin sack lining clinging to his back and legs like a spider web. He coughed to breathe before he stood up and, walking like he was drunk, struggled to disconnect his umbilical cord. Once free, he leaped over his mother's hind legs and found a nipple.

Within an hour, four more piglets were born, each a mini version of its mother, with dark spots randomly scattered around their pale bodies, like someone had shaken a quill pen over them.

All but the two smallest piglets were nursing. Bruce placed them in a cardboard box, and we brought them to the house to warm them over a heat vent. When they were livelier, Bruce returned them to their mother. An hour later, he crawled into bed, shivering from the walk from the shower to the bedroom, and I warmed him, too.

⊙ ⊙ ⊙

I finish dressing and stuff an extra pad in each side of my nursing bra before walking back into the chaos.

I don't want to bring Carlene to her father's funeral, even if she is too little to remember, so I'd asked a neighbor to watch her. Mom is showing her where we keep the diapers and bottles. Dad is warming up his car, and my older brother has started his car, too, since the seven of us won't fit in one vehicle.

It's rare for us to all be together, mostly because the farm is 200 miles away from their homes near Minneapolis. There is also a significant age difference between us. When my sister Emily was born in 1975, Marty was twenty-one, sister Debbie was nineteen, brother Matthew was nine, and I was eleven. Our relationships are largely defined by the experiences we had living under the same roof at different times.

I help Emily button her coat before I slip on mine. She puts on boots, and I choose white pumps, despite the snow. I hold her hand as we walk to Dad's car. Not that she needs help—she is seven—but I need a warm, familiar hand in mine.

CHAPTER 2

September 1981

It was a week after we decided to commit to a relationship that Bruce said he wanted me to meet his parents.

"Oh, I don't know," I said. "I'm not sure I'm ready."

"They'll love you!" he assured me. "Just like I do."

"You do?"

He pulled me to him and kissed me. "Yes, I'm sure of it."

The following week, on a crisp, sunny day, I went to meet his parents. During the four-hour drive from Minneapolis to Jasper, I thought about the only time I'd been to their farm. Bruce and I had dated earlier that summer, and by dated, I mean we went to a few parties together before making out for hours in his car. After a few weeks, he said he wanted to be "just friends," and it was while we were just friends that I drove out to the farm one night. We sat on the front stoop, his farmer-pale legs glistening in the moonlight, and he told me he would take over the farm when his parents retired in a few years.

Since it was possible I might live on their farm one day, I paid close attention to the surroundings as I drove down the quarter-mile driveway. There was a cornfield to my right, its stalks turning fall brown, and a pasture on my left, lined by barbed wire, with boulders peeking out of the ground like mountaintops. A creek ran through the middle of the pasture, and dozens of brown and black cows and last spring's calves were either grazing or lying in the green grass.

The driveway was rough, so I reached out a hand to secure the German chocolate cake riding shotgun. I'd made it that morning, hoping to impress his mother.

When I parked in front of the house, no one was in the yard.

A dozen baby pigs were running free and, thinking they'd escaped, I chased them back into the pen where their mothers were. But they scooted out from under the fence again and chased each other at breakneck speed.

I don't know how long he'd been watching, but when I turned around, Bruce was standing on the front stoop, laughing.

"They won't go anywhere," he said. "They know where the food is."

In the kitchen, Bruce and his parents, Walt and Eileen, were having coffee, which I learned later was called lunch, a light midafternoon meal that included a dessert and sometimes a sandwich. Bruce took the cake from my hands and placed it on the counter.

"Mmmm, my favorite," he whispered in my ear. "Thank you."

He turned to his parents.

"Mom, Dad, this is Lynn," he said and pulled out a chair for me.

"It's nice to meet you," his mother said and poured me a cup of coffee. I didn't like coffee, and especially not black, but I would drink it that day.

His father didn't look up from his cup. "Bruce says you're from the city."

It seemed an odd way to greet a stranger, but when Bruce didn't say anything, I had to say something.

"Well, yes, I live there now." Our family had moved to Plymouth, a suburb of Minneapolis, four years earlier, when I was fourteen. "My dad used to own the grocery store in town, though."

Walt scowled. "I never go to town."

His mother laughed nervously and placed a chocolate chip cookie on my plate.

"How was your trip? You must be tired. Would you like to lay down for a bit?" she asked, all in one breath.

I smiled and took a bite of the cookie. "Thank you, Mrs. Bouwman, this is really good." And it was. "I'm fine, though. I don't mind the drive. At least when it's not snowing!"

"Oh, call me Eileen!"

The mood lightened a little, and Bruce squeezed my thigh under the table.

Walt grabbed a toothpick and stood up. He wasn't as tall as Bruce, and he was almost completely bald. He had a weathered face, the kind you'd expect of someone who'd worked outdoors all his life. Age spots and dark hair covered his tanned arms, and his legs bowed a little.

"Time for chores," he snapped, and I nearly dropped my cup.

"I'll be out in a minute," Bruce answered.

When Walt left, Eileen seemed to relax. While she sipped her coffee, I took in her appearance. She had a small, sharp-tipped nose and creamy soft cheeks that reminded me of my grandma Signe's, and with emerging gray roots, it was clear she dyed her hair black.

"I didn't realize you lived by Bertha and Norman," I said, referring to my dad's aunt and uncle who used to own the farm near the highway.

"My brother John owns the place now," Bruce said.

"Hunh. I didn't know that," I said. "I used to go target shooting there with my dad."

"They were such nice neighbors," Eileen said. "I wish I'd learned more sign language so I could talk to them better."

"Me, too," I said.

Bruce pulled away from the table. "I'd better get outside."

I stood up, too. "I'm staying with Signe this weekend, and I told her I'd be at her place by four. Thank you for the coffee, Eileen. I hope I see you again soon!"

"Stop out anytime," she said.

Bruce walked me to my car, and we made plans to go out for dinner.

"I'll pick you up at six." He leaned in to kiss me as Walt walked across the yard toward the barn.

"Goodbye!" I called out.

Walt gave a quick one-hand wave without looking up.

"Maybe it's not your mom I need to impress," I said.

Bruce shrugged. "Don't worry about it. I'll see you tonight."

⊙ ⊙ ⊙

Over the next few months, Bruce and I alternated visits. He'd come to Plymouth one weekend, and I'd go to Jasper the next. On the weekends that I went to see him, I was allowed to sleep upstairs in the bedroom adjacent to Bruce's, the one above Walt and Eileen's, the one with the bed with squeaky metal springs, a sure way of knowing I was alone.

Alcohol was expressly forbidden in their house, but since Walt and Eileen never came upstairs, Bruce kept a bottle of Seagram's in his dresser. We slept apart, but that didn't stop us from being together, often and quietly. Other than that, we lived by the rules.

When Bruce and his father were outside working, Eileen and I would sometimes play gin rummy while she schooled me on their extensive family tree. Eileen had two sisters, and one of those sisters had twelve children. Walt had thirteen brothers and sisters, and there were dozens of children between them. Bruce was the youngest of Walt and Eileen's five children, and at that time, they had fourteen grandchildren.

Eileen never let me help in the kitchen, even though her meals were not much different than the ones I learned to make while growing up—mostly meat and potatoes, sometimes a hotdish.

Before every meal, except for midafternoon lunch, Walt

recited the Lord's Prayer, and afterward, he offered a prayer in a mix of English and Dutch, always in a humble cadence, far different than his usual bark and fuss. I asked Bruce what the words were to that prayer that seemed to take his father to his knees three times a day. He said he didn't know, and he never asked.

Bruce's grandparents had emigrated from the Netherlands and were members of the Dutch Reformed Church. The family went to church twenty miles away in a town called Edgerton because there were no Reformed churches in Jasper. I didn't know anything about the Reformed church except for what Bruce told me, mainly that members didn't work (other than to do chores) or purchase anything on Sundays.

In addition to living in the city, Walt didn't like that I was four years younger than Bruce or that I was Lutheran, even though his son John had "converted" to Lutheranism when he got married, and his daughter was married to a Church of God minister. Walt didn't even like the way I buttered toast, and he scolded me one morning at breakfast.

"This is how you do it," he said, as if I was about to put a fork in an outlet for the tenth time. He grabbed a piece of toast and flipped it one side to the other before settling on a side. "See that? That's the cut side."

Isn't every side a cut side? I thought, but I kept my mouth shut, and so did Bruce.

When we were engaged a few days before Christmas, Bruce's mother was delighted, but Walt was loath to accept it.

"You don't know anything about farm life," he reminded me for the twentieth time.

"He'll come around," Bruce assured me later, but I remained skeptical.

☉ ☉ ☉

Plans for a May 29 wedding and a honeymoon in the Poconos turned into an April 3 wedding and a night at the Holiday Inn in Sioux Falls when I learned I was pregnant. Bruce and I only told our parents and a few close friends and explained the change in date to others as a conflict with the farming schedule. People could do the math later.

As we predicted, my parents were fine with it, Eileen was politely pissed, and Walt treated me like he'd been right all along, that I was ruining his son's life.

On a Sunday in late February, Bruce and I were upstairs working on wedding plans when I felt a small cramp in my lower abdomen. I went into the bathroom and found a spot of blood on my underwear.

When I told Bruce what was happening, he didn't know what to do any more than I did, so he suggested I ask his mother. I'd rather have sat on an electric fence, but I went down to the kitchen where his parents were having coffee with Walt's brother and sister-in-law.

"Can I talk to you?" I whispered in Eileen's ear. She excused herself and followed me to the living room.

Eileen was visibly uncomfortable when I told her what was happening.

"I don't know what to do," I said. "I . . ."

"I've heard that can happen the first few months," she interrupted, opening the cupboard near the phone.

"Did it happen to you?"

She handed me a phone book. "Call the hospital," she said and rejoined her guests.

Bruce was born in Pipestone County Hospital. So was my sister Emily. But all I could think about was death. Both of my grandfathers died there. One—Signe's husband and my dad's father—from a botched appendectomy when he was only thirty-six. My great-grandmother Mathilda died there, too. The last time I saw her, I was eight years old. The woman I'd remembered—the one with the generous lap and beautiful long gray hair pinned in a bun, who kept pink wintergreen lozenges in a bowl on her coffee table—didn't exist anymore. She didn't remember anyone and only spoke Norwegian, even though she was fluent in English.

When Mathilda died, I felt grief for the first time, only I didn't know it had a name. I was told that I felt sad because someone I loved was gone and wasn't coming back, but they also said that Mathilda was old and that's what happened to old people. Now, I felt a similar sadness in addition to fear. In three weeks, I'd grown to love the idea of our mother-father-child dynamic, even if it wasn't something we'd planned. With it now in jeopardy, I didn't know what to do with my feelings except sink into them.

"Maybe it's nothing," Bruce offered, tapping the gearshift.

"No, it's something," I said, biting a nail.

At the hospital, I didn't know the right questions to ask the male doctor parked between my legs. Only one other doctor—the woman who told me I was pregnant—had ever looked around down there before. After the exam, he told me I was still pregnant but that my body was going to do what it needed to do. Whether that was to stay pregnant or not, he didn't know. Call, he said, if I experienced any more bleeding.

It was after midnight when we returned to the farm. By 5 a.m., it was clear my body was not going to remain pregnant. We went back to the hospital, and I was admitted. A few hours later, with one more excruciating cramp, it was over.

A nurse quickly wrapped up the blood-soaked pads and told us the doctor had scheduled a D&C for later that morning. I asked her what that meant, and she explained it was to clean out any debris left in my uterus. Debris, like we were discussing the remains of a house torn apart by a tornado, suggesting nothing of the life that once lived inside.

"These things happen," she said, as if that was how I was supposed to think about it, too.

Even Bruce, as I sobbed on his shoulder, said, "It wasn't meant to be."

It. Thing. Is that all this was?

The pregnancy wasn't viable or obviously I would still be pregnant, I understood that, but that's not what I needed to hear. I wanted someone to cry with me, to be sad with me.

Bruce was holding my hand when I woke up from the D&C. He said everything was fine and that he was going home and would be back after chores. Eileen came to visit in the afternoon. She brought me a jar of peanuts and said nothing about the baby. The peanuts seemed strange at the time, and they still do, but she showed up, which I would learn later was really more than I should expect from anyone when something I love dies.

When I was discharged the next morning, Bruce took me back to the farm to recover—a recovery that lasted five minutes.

While I settled under a blanket on the squeaky bed, Walt rapped on the door at the foot of the stairs.

"Bruce!" he barked. "Get down here!"

Minutes later, Bruce came back to my room looking like he'd been taken out to the woodshed. "Dad said since we don't have to get married now, maybe we should wait."

I'd believed him when he told me his father would come around, that he would learn to accept me, maybe even love me, so it took me a second to process what he said.

"Is . . ." I struggled to form words, any words. "Is that what you want?"

"I . . . I don't know . . ."

Anger mushroomed up through my body.

"Is that what you want?" I asked again.

He hung his head.

I threw back the blanket, like someone had set the bed on fire, and stood up. Lightheaded, I looked straight into his eyes.

"Fuck you!"

Walt was still at the foot of the stairs. "We don't talk like that in this house!"

I stomped over to the railing. "Shut up! I do!"

I took off my engagement ring and threw it down the stairs. "You can have it!"

I flung my suitcase on the bed and started to pack while Walt continued to yell God knows what while Bruce repeatedly called to him to calm down.

"We were engaged before I got pregnant! What changed?"

"Don't go," he said. "You need to rest."

Suitcase in hand, I stopped at the top of the stairs.

"Is this what you want?" I asked a final time. "Because if it is, you won't see me again."

He looked away. "I don't know."

I desperately wanted to drive far away. My car was right there, parked at the edge of the driveway, a 1974 bare-bones, hard-top, four-speed Mustang that would have made a fantastic exit, peeling out on the gravel, leaving a trail of dust in its wake. But between my disoriented anger and the pain pill I'd taken, I knew I shouldn't drive.

"I need you to take me to town."

At the foot of the stairs, I brushed past Walt, who was still yammering on about how his son didn't need to marry me and that I had a potty mouth, and walked through the living room. I looked over to their bedroom and saw Eileen sitting on her bed, crying.

"You can have your baby boy back," I hissed. "That's what you want, isn't it?"

I stormed out the door and waited for Bruce in his car. He

came out a few minutes later and held out my engagement ring.

"Here, please take it," he said. I tossed it in my purse.

"Drop me off at Jeanine's," I said. Jeanine was supposed to be one of my bridesmaids, but now I'd have to tell her to return the dress.

We didn't talk on the brief drive to town. By the time we pulled up to Jeanine's, I'd calmed down and was trying not to cry. Bruce put his hand on my thigh.

"I think we should talk to David," he said. "He can help us figure this out."

David was the pastor of the Lutheran church who was going to marry us. He was unlike any pastor I knew. He swore, drank wine, and had a wicked sense of humor. That Bruce wanted us to talk to David meant he hadn't given up on us, and as mad and confused as I was, I was also relieved. I loved Bruce more than anything. His father couldn't change that.

I didn't answer right away, afraid I'd keep saying the wrong thing.

Finally, I said, "Do you want me to call him?"

"Would you?" Bruce took my hand. "I'll come back to town whenever he can see us. I really do love you."

"Okay. But I need a nap first."

It was true that I needed a nap, but my mind ached more than my body. I'd never felt so angry, let alone lost control like that. It was like I was watching me be someone else. My mother, perhaps.

Mom was prone to mood swings. What didn't upset her one day would throw her into rage on another. As kids, we learned to read a few signs, like if we came home from school and smelled bread or cookies baking, it meant Mom was probably in a good mood. If the house was quiet, we knew to tread lightly.

Whether she was angry in general or angry at one of us in particular, she'd come at us full force—sometimes verbally, sometimes by ignoring us for days, and sometimes in a letter that she'd leave on the counter when she'd run away, blaming us for making her leave.

I didn't know how to talk through conflict. I only knew how to yell through it. Once, when I was a server at Country Kitchen, a man with six kids left me a quarter tip. I didn't consider that maybe the meal was all he could afford or that he was distracted and forgot to put a real tip down or that I might have been culpable in some way. Nope. All I knew was that I got ripped off. I marched into the kitchen and threw the quarter at the cook.

"It must've been your cooking because it wasn't my service!" I yelled.

My reaction stunned us both.

What happened at the farm went beyond stun. It scared me, and I feared it scared Bruce. When he said he didn't know what he wanted, I didn't consider that he, too, had suffered a loss and was struggling—right or wrong—to make his father happy. I heard what I thought I heard, internalized what may or may not have been intended, and acted from a place where reason and kindness fell away, without acknowledging that each of us that morning behaved selfishly.

I didn't take a nap. I didn't take a break at all. I strategized and worried. I needed to make things right. Apologize, beg for mercy if I had to, anything to convince him that angry was not who I was. It was a fluke, the hormones. It was all my fault.

⊙ ⊙ ⊙

Six weeks later, despite a snowstorm the night before that kept a few people away, Bruce and I were married as planned. Before we exchanged our vows, I saw Walt dab his eyes with a handkerchief. When we'd met with David after the miscarriage, I promised Bruce that I would do my best to not react if Walt made any further offhanded remarks, but watching the man cry at his son's wedding, I felt the weight of Walt's disappointment and girded myself for more conflict.

⊙ ⊙ ⊙

Bruce and I rented a house on a mostly inactive farm five miles from town—a small two-story with a pitched roof and dormer window, hardwood floors, and a staircase with a simple oak banister. There was no shower, just a large clawfoot tub. The water was so hard that we needed to add half a box of Calgon each time we took a bath just to feel clean. We hosted parties, got food poisoning on Easter after eating the church breakfast, adopted two kittens we named Festus and Miss Kitty to manage the mouse population, and went dancing on Saturday nights at the VFW.

Living near Jasper again, I felt reunited with an intangible part of myself that had stayed behind when our family moved to Plymouth. Changing schools halfway through ninth grade and going from well-known to unknown overnight felt like I'd jumped in ice water. I was one step behind everyone in my new school, an outsider in country-girl clothes. I hid my social awkwardness by staying as quiet and unseen as possible, and I followed along like I knew what I was doing. (With nine flute players in the band, no one noticed whether I was playing or not.)

I couldn't hide my academic awkwardness. None of my classes from Jasper aligned with the schedule at my new school. Instead of earth science, civics, and home ec, I was enrolled in chemistry, economics, and woodshop. I couldn't keep up, my grades plummeted, and my intellectual confidence was swallowed up by the thousand other kids, who I assumed were smarter than me, walking the halls.

High school wasn't much better. While I'd made friends, I still struggled academically. I didn't understand, or at least I didn't try to understand, most math beyond basic algebra, and after a disastrous fetal pig dissection in which I flung the corpse into the hallway, I avoided science.

Halfway through my senior year, I still had no idea what I wanted to do with my life. I thought I was destined to drift unmoored through the years with no passion or talent. Then, in a creative writing class, I met the poet Natalie Goldberg. Her first collection of poems, *Chicken and in Love*, was one of our texts, and one day, she'd come to our class to talk about poetry and to critique our poems. She liked one of mine and encouraged me to write more. I decided right then that I was going to be a writer.

I made an appointment to see one of the school's three guidance counselors to talk about college. I'd met one of them the year before when he needed volunteers to offer peer mentoring to students returning to school after drug rehab. He was a nice guy, probably a hippy in the '60s. He sought me out because I'd been caught smoking pot in the school parking lot and was threatened with detention. If I volunteered to be a mentor, my sentence would be commuted. I volunteered, but the program never got off the ground, and no one said anything further about my offense.

I didn't get an appointment with him, though. I got an even older guy with thinning gray hair and a ring around his shirt collar.

While he stroked his chin and looked through my file, I told him about Natalie Goldberg and how excited I was that I'd finally found the thing I would do the rest of my life.

When I was done talking, he said, "Lynn, you're bright. Your preliminary SAT scores were very good. You just don't apply yourself."

He was right. My best grades were in band and English, but they couldn't save my two-point-six grade point average.

"I just don't think your grades are good enough for college."
He took off his glasses and stretched back in his chair. "Have you
considered getting married?"

I was seventeen, and it wasn't the 1950s, but I said nothing
other than to thank him for his time.

I walked out of his office feeling strangely liberated. Whatever
I would do next, I decided I would do it near Jasper, where I knew
my friends would welcome me back. I made a plan to live and work
in nearby Sioux Falls, and even though I wouldn't be eighteen for
two months, my parents didn't object. For graduation, they gave
me a set of baby-blue Samsonite luggage, and I netted $500 from
family and friends, enough for a deposit on a furnished apartment
and a month's rent. I packed the luggage with clothes and the
teddy bear Dad gave me for Christmas, grabbed my ticket for the
Styx concert in Sioux Falls the following week, and drove away.

I didn't expect to be married a year later, but being married
didn't replace my dream of going to college. I would work that
out somehow, someday. At the moment, Bruce was my life,
Jasper was my home, and I was certain I'd never be an outsider
again.

⊙ ⊙ ⊙

Six months later, Walt and Eileen closed on a house in Luverne,
a town twenty miles away, and, per the Bouwman family plan,
Bruce and I moved to the farm.

I was four months pregnant.

The farmhouse was decorated in early-1970s heavy gold
curtains and thatch-pattern kitchen carpet, which I couldn't wait
to swap out for blinds and tile. Eileen, however, wasn't ready to
let go of the only home she'd known for forty years and cautioned
me against changing anything, so the mishmash furniture and

other items Bruce and I accumulated had to make the place bend more to our taste: my piano, a kitchen cabinet we repurposed as a changing table, a large antique mirror, and the headboard and dresser Bruce made before we were married. Even the hideous avocado-colored lamp we'd received as a wedding gift and the wildly floral secondhand pullout couch helped lighten up the dark, castle-like feel of the golden living room, the eternal autumn.

Walt embraced retirement the same way Eileen embraced changing curtains. He didn't. He was still a farmer, by God, and he came to the farm almost every weekday.

He bought a Chevy Chevette, the color of a banana, to drive the forty-mile round trip to save on gas. From the kitchen window, I had a clear view of the highway, so it wasn't hard to miss his bright yellow car buzzing down the road. My stomach always flipped when he pulled into the yard. While he was there, he either barked my name when he needed something or ignored me. If he muttered a thank-you after our noon meal, it was always into the air.

Bruce never confronted his father, opting instead to keep me from losing my cool. I didn't make that easy, although I kept my promise to never again raise my voice to Walt. As Bruce always reminded me, "One of you has to be the adult." He never lost faith that one day his father would "come around."

Walt was right about one thing. I didn't know anything about farming, especially the emotional component, which I hadn't considered.

Bruce taught me how to feed and water the pigs and cattle, but he warned me to not get attached. I didn't understand what he meant until Walt, John, and John's son Jason came to the farm to wean and sterilize calves.

Bruce and Walt drove the old three-on-the-tree Ford into the pasture followed by John and Jason on three-wheelers and our dog, a German shepherd named Duke. They'd made me the gatekeeper, so I closed the gate and waited for them to return. Geese flew overhead. The sound of combines harvesting beans hummed softly in the distance. The wind rustled through the drying cornfields. Crows disappeared into the stalks.

Then, all hell broke loose.

Bruce raced up in the truck, followed by 200 confused cows and calves. He slammed on the brakes and got out of the truck. He and the dog separated the calves and moved them toward the gate while his father, brother, and nephew kept the cows back. I opened the gate, and Bruce guided the calves through the yard. After John, Walt, and Jason were through, I shut the gate as the cows paced back and forth along the fence, raising their heads and bellowing.

By the time I got to the stockyard, John was clamping the male calves' legs between iron rails. Systematically, he cut off their scrotums and tossed them to the dog. The calves' eyes were wild as they tossed and bucked in their confinement. Once released, they huddled against the fence and bawled to their mothers.

The cows' wailing was deafening, and it continued throughout the night. I laid awake thinking about what we'd done. I whispered to Bruce that no one would come after me in a pickup truck to separate me from our baby. He mumbled something about how it was impossible to compare a human with a cow. I silently disagreed. The cows were grieving the same as any mother would.

When I went outside to start chores the next morning, a few cows were still calling to their calves, their voices hoarse and strained. I walked past the stockyard where the newly weaned calves stood silently in the dirt, their big eyes following me as I disappeared into the silo room. For a moment, I thought about opening the gates and letting them run to their mothers. Instead, I turned on the conveyor and watched silage pour into the trough.

⊙ ⊙ ⊙

On my due date, March 10, my doctor told me the baby wouldn't be born for another few weeks if she had her way.

"Your blood pressure is high. The baby is big enough," he said, taking off his gloves. "Time to get it out."

"Okay," I said, like I knew what he meant.

When he left the room, I got dressed, and a nurse came in with some papers. She told me I would need them to check into the hospital.

"Now?" I asked.

"Yes. They're waiting for you."

Bruce met me at the coatrack.

"So, what did he say?" he asked cheerfully, helping me into my coat. Bruce was terribly excited to meet the baby. Every night, he rubbed my belly like it was Aladdin's lamp. "Come out and play!" he'd say.

"I have to go to the hospital," I said quietly. "He said the baby has to be born soon."

Bruce took one of my hands, and I clutched the papers with the other. We walked across the icy parking lot, and he helped me into the car.

He started the car as I read over the papers. My heart pulsed in my temples.

"I don't know what any of this means!" I slapped the papers. "I don't know what they're going to do! Am I having a C-section? Is the baby okay?"

Bruce took a deep breath. "Let's just sit here for a minute."

"But they're expecting us at the hospital! We have to go!"

He rubbed my knee. "They'll be there when we get there. We need some time to think."

I was afraid and so was he, but we were afraid together. I loosened my death grip on the papers.

When we felt ready to go, as was always Bruce's positive approach to life, he said, "We're having a baby!" which we did, the next day, at 7:27 in the evening after more than thirteen hours of induced labor.

Walt and Eileen came to the hospital the next day.

"She looks like a Bouwman," Walt said, like he had doubts, although he did seem happy to meet his new granddaughter. He didn't hold her, but he held her hand gingerly in his large, calloused hand and smiled when her fingers closed around his finger.

"See?" Bruce said after they left. "He's coming around."

⊙ ⊙ ⊙

They were sitting on folding chairs when I walked into the funeral home. Walt was slumped over, his hands folded on his lap. When he saw me, he shook his head.

I was expecting him to say something like if Bruce hadn't married me, if we hadn't had a baby, if I had just gone away when he told me to, his son would be alive. Instead, he mumbled, "We should have sold cattle. We should have sold cattle."

Walt and Bruce had planned to take a load of steers to the stockyards in Sioux Falls on Tuesday, but Walt called Monday night and said he'd changed his mind, that they would go later in the week. But Bruce died on Tuesday, and in Walt's mind, if they'd sold cattle, Bruce would still be alive.

Before I could say that it wasn't his fault, Eileen grabbed my hand, and I sat down next to her.

"He's dead," she said flatly.

I nodded.

She was shaking so hard, and her pulse was racing so fast, I feared she would have a stroke. She didn't say much as we planned the funeral except to insist on the most durable casket and that the song "How Great Thou Art" be included in the service.

Someone suggested Psalm 23 for the back of the service folder, but I was looking for answers more than comfort.

"Wasn't that song . . ." I started singing The Byrd's "Turn! Turn! Turn!" "Wasn't that in the Bible, like in Leviticus? Deuteronomy? It's somewhere in the Old Testament, right?"

"Ecclesiastes," said the funeral director as he paged through his Bible. "'For everything there is a season, and a time for every matter under the heaven: a time to be born, and a time to die; a time to plant, and a time to pluck up what is planted; a time to kill, and a time to heal; a time to break down, and a time to build up; a time to weep, and a time to laugh; a time to mourn, and a time to dance.'"

"It wasn't meant to be," I remembered Bruce said after the miscarriage.

"That's the one," I said.

No one objected.

When the arrangements were complete, Eileen loosened her grip, and we stood up to leave. I hugged her and left her in the care of her daughter. I walked over to Walt and hugged him, too.

"See you tomorrow," I said. He nodded.

The next day at the viewing—a misnomer since there was nothing to view except a brown casket adorned in brass—Walt motioned for me to sit next to him. He offered his hand.

"I'm . . ." he said. "I'm a fool."

I squeezed his hand and stared at the casket.

"I said things . . ."

He was silent for a few moments as he collected his thoughts.

"I hurt Bruce, I know."

He took a deep breath and continued.

"I can't take it back."

I wanted to tell him everything was fine, but that wouldn't have been true.

"I am going to spend the rest of my life making it up to Carlene. And to you." He wiped away a tear. "I love that little girl. You are always welcome in our home."

Walt, it seemed, had finally come around.

CHAPTER 3

I don't know why Dad decided to take the direct route to Jasper, today of all days. I've been there twice since they told me Bruce died, but each time, I took the long way—a half-mile west, two miles north, one mile east—crossing the tracks in town, the ones with the flashing lights. There isn't even a stop sign at the tracks where Bruce died, the ones over the dirt road. Not that anyone would pay attention to a stop sign. Everyone knows the tracks are there.

As we cross, I look out the window, hoping to see something that would suggest a train-tractor collision, something that would make Bruce's death real and not hearsay. Other than boot prints in the snow in the ditch, the crossing looks the same, and as we jostle about on the washboard road, I wonder, *How did Bruce not hear a train?*

He was hauling two empty gravity boxes which, counter to their name, bounce as though weightless even when full. *Was he paying attention to them instead of the tracks?*

A few weeks before Carlene was born, I was sitting on the couch watching TV when I suddenly felt cold. Not chilly cold. An ominous cold. The baby was kicking, but the feeling didn't seem related to her. It was about Bruce. *But why?* He was in town at play practice before bowling with his league. There was nothing dangerous in that.

I got up to turn the channel, and the feeling grew more urgent, so, ridiculous or not, I called the bowling alley.

"Hey, this is Lynn Bouwman. Is Bruce there?"

"Hi, honey! Yeah, he's here. I'll get him."

A minute later, Bruce picked up the phone. "Hey, hon!"

"Hi. Um, I know this sounds stupid, but would you come home?"

"What's wrong? Is the baby alright?"

"Yes, just . . . please come home."

"Sure, I'll be right there."

Five minutes later, I heard a train whistle.

Before we were married, we were driving back to the farm after a wedding dance on a night so foggy we couldn't see the ditch on either side of the road. Bruce stopped several feet from the tracks and rolled down his window to listen for a train. After several seconds of quiet, we crossed safely. I remembered feeling relieved, like we'd cheated death.

Pacing the living room, I heard the whistle again, this time so close that I knew it was near or at the intersection. Bruce had to be at the tracks by then, and I was convinced that, acting on an obtuse feeling, I had killed him. I was sobbing and nearly sick to my stomach when a few minutes later, I saw his headlights on the garage door.

He walked in the door, and I threw my arms around him. "I thought you were dead!"

"I'd have been here sooner, but there was a train," he said, chuckling. "Why are you shaking? Honey, I'm fine."

We moved to the couch, and I lay with my head in his lap. He stroked my hair, and we talked about death and what we would want for the other if one of us died because, you know, that was never going to happen. He said he'd want me to move on. I told him he wasn't allowed to marry any of his former girlfriends.

When David and John showed up at my door three days ago, their eyes swollen from tears, I knew before they said it: the train whistle I heard while I was folding diapers was meant for Bruce.

CHAPTER 4

At the church, chairs are set up in the hallway for the overflow crowd. With hundreds of sad eyes watching, I walk down the aisle with my parents behind the pallbearers.

Almost a year ago, many of those same eyes watched me walk down that same aisle, holding on to Dad's arm as Bruce—tall, handsome, and full of life—waited for me at the altar. Now, he lies dead in a casket covered in a spray of lilies, carnations, and roses with a small red ribbon attached, scrolled with the word "Daddy."

Except for a few muffled cries, the mourning congregation is stoic, and so am I. While they sing "Children of the Heavenly Father," I stare at the casket and remember when Bruce sang it at his former church a few months ago. It's not his performance I think about, though. It's how, on our way to Edgerton that dull, gray Sunday morning, Elton John's "Funeral for a Friend" came on the radio, and we sang it all the way to the church.

Years before he knew I existed, when I was in eighth grade and he was a senior, Bruce played Curly in the Jasper High School production of *Oklahoma!* I was starstruck, mesmerized by his voice, and for the rest of the year, I was his unknown groupie. I attended all of his choir concerts, even though it pained me to see another girl sit on his knee during a performance of "Ticket to Ride." When we'd formally met at the Styx concert a few weeks after I graduated, I couldn't believe it when he said he hoped he'd see me again, the awkward girl from the third row of the high school auditorium who couldn't carry a tune if it was strapped around her waist. But whenever we listened to music, I sang along with him like I was Barbra Streisand.

[44]

The hymn ends and the church is quiet except for the sound of one person crying. It is my father, fully engaged in shoulder-shaking, head-in-hands, inconsolable sobbing. My mother thrusts a tissue at him and scolds him with a sharp, "Shhhh!"

Dad was six years old when his father died, and now his only grandchild is fatherless. He has earned the right to cry.

I imagine liberating my own pain that way or throwing myself on Bruce's casket and wailing, but what would people think? What would my mother say? My only emotional emancipation happens after the funeral, in the hallway, when I think no one is looking. I kiss my hand and touch his casket, like I'm saying goodbye to a clandestine lover.

I pull my coat from the hanger and slip it on as I walk out of the church to the black Chrysler parked behind the hearse. The clouds are heavy. More snow will fall soon.

The driver opens the passenger door.

"Thank you," I say, and slide to the center of the seat to make room for my grandmother Katinka while Signe and my parents file into the back seat. Hot air blasts on my bare legs, and I reach out to turn down the fan as the driver eases into the driver's seat.

I look away as the pallbearers wheel the casket to the back of the hearse. When I shift in the seat to pull a tissue out of my coat pocket, I feel the pull of the stitches between my legs. It was a difficult birth, but she came out perfect. All nine pounds of her. Ten fingers, ten toes, and her father's Charlie Brown head.

I dab my eyes and look up as they close the hearse door. For three days, I've been an actor reciting lines: "Yes, I agree, this is a very tragic loss." "I'll let you know. Thank you for your concern." "We'll be fine. How are you?" But right now, all I'm thinking is, *This is it. I'll never be this close to his body ever again. And he's all alone. He's all alone!* I want to sneak into the back of the hearse, open his casket, climb in, and close the lid, but if I say this out loud, they'll call me crazy. They'll say he's dead; he doesn't know he's alone.

Torn up and screaming inside, I stare straight ahead as the procession of cars starts its way down the main street of town. When the hearse is halfway across the railroad tracks, the crossing lights begin to flash. The rest of the procession will have to wait. The irony is as heavy as the silence as we continue the journey to the cemetery.

It begins to snow, and another train passes as David prays over the casket. I look up and see a childhood friend watching me from across the crowd of bowed heads. His helpless look mirrors my own, and we stare at each other for the remainder of the prayer, sustaining me like a weight-bearing wall.

Back in the Chrysler, the others chat while I wonder if I have enough emotional energy to get through the luncheon.

"Would you take me home?" I don't ask the driver.

◉ ◉ ◉

Standing up from the table at the front of the church social hall, I leave a ham sandwich and a scoop of macaroni salad untouched on my plate. A line of mourners has formed around the perimeter of the long, brightly lit room that smells of waxed floors and Folgers. Low-voiced conversations hum in the background as members of the Ladies Aid wash dishes in the kitchen. I've worked these luncheons before alongside my grandmothers, my aunt Mavis, and former teachers whom I never called by their first names.

Church wasn't a place as much as it was something I did, and growing up, I did a lot of church: Sunday school, catechism, choir, youth group. I had to have a really good excuse not to do church. When I married Bruce, I didn't consider that I had a choice about church, and since Bruce grew up doing church, too, we did church together. He sang in the choir and taught Sunday school, and I did Ladies Aid.

The line of mourners starts to advance. While the first in line shake hands with Walt and Eileen and my parents, I straighten my shirt, pull the hem of my skirt below my knees, and cross my jacket across my chest. While the pads have held up, I really need to see Carlene soon.

After a few hundred quickly shared memories, offers of sympathy, and sometimes painful hugs, it is time to go home. My sister Debbie says she wants to buy some wine while we are in town and that she needs cash for her trip home. I tell Dad to stop at the municipal bar downtown since they sell bottles from behind the counter and allow customers to write a check twenty dollars above the purchase amount.

Debbie and I walk into the dimly lit bar. Several patrons, some of whom were at the funeral, watch us and say nothing.

"Hey, Lynn," says the bartender.

"Hey. Can we get a bottle of rosé?" I ask. "And will you take my sister's out-of-town check?"

"Not a problem," he says, reaching for the wine. He makes a funny comment about cheap wine, and both Debbie and I laugh, a normal, ordinary moment that isn't missed by the ears at the bar.

At home, Carlene is asleep, so I go into the bathroom to pump my engorged left breast and what I can from the right one, which is still painful in the area of the blocked duct. I tuck a warm compress under my right arm and secure it with my bra, throw on Bruce's South Dakota State University shirt, and join my family and David in the living room. David has kept a close eye on me the last few days.

There is a stack of cards in a basket on the coffee table. I put a pillow on the floor, sit down, and begin to open them. Cash and checks fall out of many of them.

"Why are people giving me money?" I ask.

"It's for a memorial," someone explains.

There are hymnals in our church with a sticker inside dedicated to the loving memory of someone. Is that what I am supposed to do? Buy hymnals?

I read the sympathy cards like they're Tarot cards.

"Time heals all wounds," I say to David, waving a few in the air.

David shakes his head. He knows my pain is white-hot. He also knows I'm impatient. When Bruce and I went to see him after the miscarriage, he reminded me several times to let Bruce process his thoughts whenever I pressed him for answers. I hate surprises, I'd told them. Especially the emotional ones.

"Time doesn't heal," David says. "It only gives us perspective."

I put the cards down.

"Time doesn't have the power to heal," he continues. "Healing implies it goes away. But years from now, you'll be able to recall this time and feel everything you feel at this moment. In time, you will get stronger, you will feel joy again, you will build yourself up, but this comes from inside you, not because a certain amount of time passes. It's a lot of work, and you won't be the same person you were before he died. You can't be."

Years from now? Is he kidding me? I never want to feel this way again: exposed, raw, and so naive. And I won't, I decide. I'll show David just how wrong he is.

CHAPTER 5

I wake up and bury my face in Bruce's pillow and breathe in the faint scent of his hair and skin. After what feels like a five-day hurricane, Carlene and I are alone. Except for a refrigerator filled with sandwich meat, fruit salad, and leftover hot dishes, the house is physically back to its pre-death state. The folding chairs are in the basement, and someone, probably my dad, who needed to stay busy, vacuumed and took the trash to the burn pile. The laundry is folded and put away. Bruce's clothes hang in the closet, his contacts case sits on the bathroom counter, and his razor—with bits of his whiskers between the blades—rests next to our toothbrush holder. He could walk in any time, and things would be the same as when he left.

"Be good for mommy," he'd said to Carlene the last time we saw him. He gave her foot a little pinch before kissing me on the top of my head. "Love you."

I turn on a lamp and open the drawer of the headboard where I keep the dozens of letters and cards from Bruce. I shuffle through them until I find the first one, from the day he said he loved me, the day he said he wanted me to meet his parents:

September 20, 1981

It feels good to be home again, but I feel sad about leaving the Cities, too, because I had to leave you behind. I knew I should have tried to put you in my suitcase!

I know it's going to be hard to be apart from you for a week. At least I can think about you every day.

I've just got the happiest feeling inside. That's because

I've found this really terrific girl. She's just the best! And I'm crazy about her!

I wish you were here. I miss you already.

Love, Bruce.

Even though he said he felt like he could tell me anything, after our two-week make-out session two summers ago, Bruce largely ignored me. After I went to see him at the farm that July, I didn't see him again until September, when I was barely eking out a living waiting tables in Sioux Falls and my parents had agreed I could move home until I had a plan for what I'd do next.

Before I left, I wanted to say goodbye to friends in Jasper, so I went to a home football game with my friend Lisa. While there was a good chance I would run into Bruce, I hoped I wouldn't. I felt defeated enough without him ignoring me. Friends, he'd said. He didn't know the first thing about being my friend.

Lisa saw him first, standing on the sidelines with his best friend Curt. I watched him throughout the game, and he didn't seem to notice I was there. When the game was over, and Lisa and I were in the parking lot discussing where we'd go next, Bruce tapped me on the shoulder.

"Hi there!" he said. "How've you been?"

I'm so excited to see you! said the butterflies in my stomach, but common sense replied, "I'm okay. You?"

"Better," he said.

God, I've missed that smile. "I'm moving on Sunday," I blurted.

His smile faded. "Oh."

"Yeah, going back to Minneapolis. You know, find a better job."

He nodded.

Lisa tugged at my jacket and said it was time to go.

"Well, it was good to see you again," I said, which wasn't a lie, but at least I said it without sounding like a thirteen-year-old. "Take care."

"Yeah, you, too."

He looked hurt. I didn't care. Maybe now he knew what I felt the night he ducked into a bar rather than talk to me at the Edgerton Dutch Festival. He knew I couldn't follow him because I wasn't old enough. Not that I would have followed him anyway. That's how little he knew me. I had no desire to stalk him. But that's when I knew he didn't mean anything he'd said about being my friend. He had things to work out, things he couldn't share with me, and that was okay, but he didn't have to be a jerk about it.

Lisa drove us to a party on some dirt road in the middle of nowhere. Same crowd, same beer, but nothing felt the same. I was moving away from Jasper again, and this time, I was leaving more than the place I considered home. I was leaving Bruce, too, even though he wasn't mine to leave.

When I didn't feel better an hour later, I decided to go back to Signe's, where I was staying that night. Lisa was having fun, and I didn't want to take her away, so I asked around to see if anyone was going back to town.

"Pat's going home soon, I think," someone said.

I found him talking to my sixth-grade boyfriend and my second cousin, Dean, who teachers always assumed, because we had the same last name and looked similar, was my twin.

"Are you leaving soon?" I asked Pat.

"Yeah. Have to work tomorrow."

"Can you drop me off at my car in town?"

"Sure. Meet me in a few. I'm parked down there." He pointed into the dark. I'd find it.

Pat drove a 1969 Dodge Super Bee, but that night, instead of asking him, "How do you shift this thing?" like I did the first time I was a passenger, we sat mostly in silence. As we glided down the roads, I closed my eyes and remembered the last time I was in his car. Six of us, driving around the back roads, listening to REO Speedwagon's *Hi Infidelity,* back when life didn't feel so complicated.

Pat dropped me off at the Mustang parked a half block from downtown. As I drove toward the main street, I saw Bruce walk out of the municipal bar alone. Seeing me, he waved for me to stop.

Great. He is absolutely the last . . . oh, who am I kidding? He's the only person I want to see right now!

I rolled down my window.

"Hey, I'm glad I ran into you," he said. "Can I get in?"

"Sure, yeah." I threw an empty Wendy's bag and Mountain Dew cans in the back and shoved a half-empty bottle of vodka under the seat.

"Can we drive around a little?" he asked.

A little stretched into an hour, so I pulled in next to his car so we could keep talking without using up any more gas. While he didn't get specific about why he broke things off with me in July, he apologized more than once for hurting me. He asked if I was seeing anyone, and I told him I'd been in contact with someone I dated a few times in high school and that we might go out when I moved back.

"Can you tell him no?" he asked.

"Um . . . I think so. But why?"

"When you told me tonight that you were leaving, that tore me up."

"Hmmm. But you haven't tried to contact me all summer."

He was quiet for a moment. "I didn't realize how I felt until you said you were leaving. I was going to get your parents' phone number and call you next week to tell you what I'm telling you now."

I liked him far too much to risk asking the next question: would he have realized how he felt if he *hadn't* seen me at the game?

"A bunch of us are going to the Viking's game next Sunday," he continued. "We're driving up on Saturday and staying overnight. Can I call you?"

"Of course, you can!" I dug around in my purse for a pen. Not finding one, I told him I'd send it to him in a letter after I finished moving.

"Great!" he said, and he kissed me like he wouldn't see me for a week. "I'll call you as soon as I get there."

Carlene starts to fuss. I wipe my eyes on the corner of his pillowcase and put the letter back in the drawer.

The week before she was born, Bruce had put the crib together and set it right outside our bedroom because he wouldn't have been able to get around it from his side of the bed if we'd put it in our room. With so many people in and out of the house the day he died, my dad and brother had disassembled it and reassembled it in our bedroom since Bruce getting around it was no longer an issue.

In the last five days, Carlene hasn't asked for more than she needs, like she senses what happened. She wakes up only once a night, isn't colicky, and doesn't mind breast milk for one feeding and formula the next. Unlike her raucous, almost nonstop activity in utero, she loves to sleep.

I pick her up and bring her to bed to feed her. When she's finished, I rock us both to sleep with the gentle waves of the waterbed.

An hour later, I wake up when I hear a pickup drive into our yard. I get up, throw on some clothes, and go to the kitchen to start coffee. Then I remember Bruce isn't here. *Why am I making coffee?*

I stare out the kitchen window at a tall man in dark coveralls walking to the barn. It is John, and I know it's John, but he is wearing what Bruce would have been wearing and doing what Bruce should have been doing, and for a second, I imagine it *is* Bruce, and my heart doesn't feel like it's being rolled over broken glass.

I make a slice of toast and think about how I probably still don't butter bread the Walt way. Bruce would be touched by his father's *mea culpa*, but I also know people say a lot of things when they're hurting. Bruce would want me to give Walt's apology the benefit of the doubt, but with my trust in pieces, I resolve to remain skeptical.

I leave half of my toast on the plate and rejoin Carlene in bed.

I'm awakened again an hour later, this time by the phone. It's Bruce's brother, Doug. He says the family decided that he and his family would take over the farm since Bruce and I didn't own it, and that they would move in the following week, and oh, by the way, I am welcome to stay until I figure out where I would live next.

John is still in the barn. I march out to talk to him.

"I know I have to move, but next week?"

"I'll talk to him," John said.

Someone told me, sometime before the funeral, that no one should make any major decisions or move within six months to a year after a spouse dies. John bought me three weeks. Three weeks to pack up Bruce's things. Three weeks to pack up my things. Three weeks to say goodbye.

CHAPTER 6

Death is big news in a county of 11,000 people, and I assumed there would be at least a mention of Bruce's accident in the local newspaper. But the photos on the front page take me a minute to comprehend, like they're an optical illusion. One caption reads: "The body of Bruce Bouwman can be seen in the center of the photograph alongside the tracks and covered with a tarp."

Only, Bruce's body isn't completely covered. His boots protrude from the bottom.

In the top of the frame is his International Harvester tractor, the one they said I'd never see again, its front end nothing more than shredded, dangling metal and jagged glass. To the right is a line of anhydrous ammonia tanker cars at rest on the tracks, the same ones I'd seen from the front window.

The most disturbing thing isn't Bruce's body or the tarp or the tractor. It's that the man behind the camera and the men from the ambulance crew who fill the rest of the photo knew what I didn't know yet. They didn't tell me Bruce was dead until everything was cleaned up and hauled away. I wasn't allowed to witness the aftermath of the accident or hold Bruce's lifeless body. They denied me the chance to defend the person I love most in the world from speculation because I'm sure they were all wondering, as am I, *How did it happen? How could it happen? How do you not hear a train?*

I don't know how to feel so many things at once: angry that the paper exploited his death, sad that such a peaceful person died in such a traumatic way, and frightened by the violence in the photo. I feel like I will throw up from this convulsive crying or perhaps die from the pain.

I have to talk to someone.

"Daddy?" I cry, grasping the phone as I collapse in a heap on the floor.

"Lynnie?" he asks. "Lynnie, what's happened?"

"There . . . are . . . pictures, Dad! Pictures . . . in . . . the . . . paper! You said . . . I'd never . . . have to see . . . his tractor! You promised!"

As far as I knew, Dad hadn't seen the tractor, either, and when I'd asked him what they did with it, he'd said they told him it had been towed somewhere far away.

"Shhhh, honey, shhhh," Dad whispers.

I tell him how all week I thought Bruce had been dragged along the tracks and that was why no one let me see his body. I don't know why this matters. Dead is dead. But the shape of a body under a tarp and two boots attached to two legs makes me wonder even more, *What wasn't I allowed to see?* And I hate that I wonder about it. And I hate the thoughts I've had all week of Bruce's blood strewn around the ditch. And I hate being so angry at the people who wouldn't let me see my own husband's body.

"I have to see David," I tell Dad. David saw Bruce dead. I remember the pain in his eyes and how he hugged me until I lost my breath, like he wanted to protect me from all of it. John saw Bruce dead, too. He was the one who identified Bruce's body. Why him, I wondered at the time, when I was a half mile away. Did they think I was too fragile to handle such adult responsibility? Such pain? Such horror? "I'll call you later, Daddy."

When I'm calm enough to drive, I go to the church and find David in his office. I set Carlene's car seat on his desk and ask, "Was he in a million pieces?"

David sighs, like he knew this question was coming. "No. Bruce died from a traumatic head wound. He was thrown through the windshield and died on impact."

I'm sure my heart will beat out of my chest. "Did Bruce know he was going to die? Did he see the train in that one last second? Did he feel any pain?"

David hands me a tissue and says nothing.

"I just wish I could have touched his hand. I wish I could have said goodbye."

CHAPTER 7

Carlene is baptized in a private ceremony on Easter Sunday, April 3, which would have also been our first wedding anniversary. Afterward, David stops me on my way out the door.

"Were you in the bar on Friday?" he asks.

"No, why? Wait . . .you mean right after the funeral?"

He nods.

"My sister cashed a check. She bought some wine—"

"Well, apparently you're drinking."

"Oh, good lord . . ."

"Also, have you been to the funeral home?"

"Yes, a few days ago. I needed to pay for—"

"I know, but someone saw you go in and come out an hour later."

"So?"

"You know how people are."

"What? They think I'm sleeping with the funeral director?"

I know this town has gossips, and I knew I was being watched, but how did I go from being the poor widow with the baby to a boozy philanderer in two weeks?

David reminds me that people are going to see what they want to see and believe what they want to believe, but still, this bothers me. Jasper is my home and yet I feel it falling away, my presence relegated to the outside. I am devolving into a stranger.

Driving home, I think about a boy I knew years ago. Before we moved to Jasper, my family lived in Bloomington, a suburb of Minneapolis, where Kenny lived down the block from me. From his living room window, he watched my friends and me ride our bikes and play hide-and-seek. We whispered about him, about how weird he was, but mostly we felt sorry for him because of his mother, who never allowed him to play with us, and on the rare occasion he was outside, even on the hottest days, she made him wear a jacket.

Just before I started second grade, my parents enrolled me in a private Lutheran school because the school district's new math and sex education didn't sit well with my father. On the first day, I walked to the bus stop alone while my friends walked to the public school. Kenny's mom's powder-blue sedan was parked near the curb. He was sitting in the back seat. I'd not met them formally, so I walked past and stood next to the curb. When the bus arrived, I got in and sat behind the driver, like my mom told me to. "At least for the first few days," she'd said. "Until you make some friends." Kenny, clinging to his lunchbox, got on the bus and shuffled to the back of the bus.

Like the ride to school, there were only a few others on the bus on the ride home. No one seemed to know each other, so it was mostly quiet. Kenny's mom was parked at the bus stop. He dutifully climbed into the back seat while I walked home.

On rainy mornings, Kenny's mom would motion for me to sit in the back seat with Kenny to wait for the bus. Sometimes I did, even though I didn't like how the blue houndstooth vinyl interior smelled of mothballs and cigarette smoke. She'd stare out the window, listening to the radio, never saying a word to me or to Kenny.

A few years after we moved to Jasper, I overheard Mom and Dad talking about how Kenny's mom died by suicide and that his dad had remarried "a nice lady." Kenny, they said, was now "fine."

I wonder now if Kenny still feels as lonely as he looked walking to and from his mother's car at the bus stop. Or if, like me, he never forgets the feeling of being on the outside, and it pricks him sometimes, like a burr that gets stuck to your sock.

⊙ ⊙ ⊙

Instead of drinking champagne with Bruce to celebrate our anniversary and Carlene's baptism, like we'd planned to do before he died, I go home to a houseful of people, mostly Bruce's friends.

It was their idea to throw a party. They'd said it felt like the right way to remember and honor their friend. When they told me about it a few days after the funeral, I agreed to have it at the farm because I knew Bruce would want to do the same thing for any of them if they died.

I listen to their stories and memories of the Bruce they knew before I came along, when he was as immature as the rest of them. Most of them knew him his entire life, or at least longer than the twenty-one months that I did. They talk about fishing and road trips, and I think about how we never had the chance to take a vacation together.

I am outside of their conversation because I only knew the responsible man Bruce had become. Who wants to talk about Lamaze classes, buying a new type of pig feed, or fixing water pipes—the everyday things that shaped our life? No one, that's who. Still, as Carlene is passed from friend to friend, some of them crying as they hold her close, I'm sad for her and for me that we might never get to know them any better than we do right now.

⊙ ⊙ ⊙

It is after midnight, and everyone except Curt has gone home. The beer is gone, but I find a half-full bottle of peppermint schnapps in the cabinet next to the refrigerator. We sit on the couch, sip from the bottle, and talk.

"You know, there wouldn't have been a Bruce and me without you," I say.

I'd known Curt well enough from seeing him in church that when I'd run into him outside the former Haraldson's Grocery a few days before the Styx concert, I said hello. He saw I was using crutches and asked what happened.

"I fell down the stairs at the bar in Garretson last weekend," I explained. "I might have had a little to drink."

He said he was going to the concert with some friends and, since there was no assigned seating, he offered to save me a seat.

"That would be great!" I said. "You're a lifesaver!"

At the concert, Lisa helped me find Curt. She'd gone to the same church, so she knew who I was looking for. When we found him, I settled into my seat while he and Lisa exchanged hellos.

I scoped out the surroundings. Curt was at the end of a line of several guys I recognized, all of whom were older than me, but it was the one sitting next to him who made my heart stop for a second.

"Who is that next to you?" I whispered in Curt's ear.

"Bruce Bouwman," he said.

"That's Bruce Bouwman!" I squeaked in Lisa's ear at the same time Bruce whispered in Curt's other ear, "Who's that girl?"

I take another sip before handing the bottle to Curt. "There also wouldn't be a you and Lisa without Bruce. It was his idea to invite you guys over for dinner last summer. He thought you'd be great together. And he was right!"

We talk about the serendipitous nature of how we got to be sitting on this couch, drinking schnapps and feeling such profound loss, how if one thing had been added or taken away— if I hadn't fallen down the bowling alley stairs and broken my foot, if Curt hadn't been walking down the street when I walked out of the grocery store, if Pat hadn't gotten me back to town at the exact moment Bruce was leaving the bar—things would be different.

Good different or worse different, if that's even possible, we'll never know.

CHAPTER 8

There are several apartment complexes near my parents' house in Plymouth, and after a series of phone calls and phone applications, which takes about a week, I send a security deposit for a two-bedroom place with underground parking, a trash chute, and an outdoor pool, but none of the charm of the farm. I have no interest in replicating what I have to leave.

With the help of John's wife, Janice, I start going through Bruce's things. I'm sure I've made Janice crazy from the moment she met me. But even with all my questions about farming and cooking and all my Walt frustrations, she has never made me feel like a bother. She's just the practical, no-nonsense person I need to keep me focused right now.

I start a giveaway pile and a keep pile. In the keep pile, I add Bruce's bowling shirt, letter jacket, the ratty brown bathrobe, his SDSU T-shirt, and his International Harvester cap. In the giveaway pile are the cowboy boots I gave him last Christmas, his winter jacket, and the rest of his clothes. I keep everything he collected from high school and college, including the mug he received from his year as vice president of SDSU's Statesmen Men's Chorus, the journal he kept when he went to Europe, and the countless photos of parties and places he'd been with people he knew before me, including a photo of four guys mooning the camera. I recognize the last butt on the left.

I pack up four years of financial records Bruce had "filed" in shoeboxes under the bed. I'll go through the ones I need for taxes and the ones I can destroy after I've moved. I'd been strangely excited about filing taxes with Bruce, just like I was when we opened our joint checking account. It was such an adult thing to do.

I go through his wallet, which I gave him two Christmases ago. It's made of black cowhide and has the start of a bend in the center from the back pocket of his jeans. I find his Red Cross blood donor card, the Kama Sutra card, both of our prepaid activity cards that got us into high school basketball games and concerts, three photos of me, a scrap of paper with my parents' phone number written on it, a receipt from M&M Distributing from December 10 (*Is that where he bought the griddle he gave me for Christmas?*), and his voter registration card. Bruce was with me in November when I voted for the first time, another "adult" thing I was excited to do.

Of all the things I have to go through, Bruce's toiletries are the hardest. Sharing a bathroom with someone who wasn't my sibling was more intimate than I thought it would be. Maybe I didn't know Bruce in the same way his friends and family did, but I know how he took a shower. We'd taken many of them together. I watched him brush his teeth, shave, pee, and comb his hair, and I listened when he fussed about his receding hairline and wondered whether to grow a beard again.

Now, standing here in our bathroom, holding an empty gin box, prepared to sort and discard the things no one but me saw him use, I think how I'll never buy shampoo, toothpaste, toilet paper, and soap for us again. I'll never loop a freshly washed towel through the towel ring next to the sink. I'll never stand in front of the open closet wondering out loud what I should wear, and never again will he sidle up behind me and cup his hands around my breasts and kiss my neck and ask me if I want help deciding.

I set the box on the counter and open his drawer, the one on the left under the counter. I sift through the contents and take out his Right Guard deodorant, two razor blades, one disposable razor, a black plastic comb, and a near-full spool of dental floss, which are all crowded next to his empty travel toiletry bag. I place the dental floss and disposable razor in the gin box for me to use and toss his travel bag in the giveaway pile. The rest I put in the trash.

I take out the blue bottle of half-full Cool Water. Bruce was frugal, but when it came to cologne, he dug a little deeper in his pockets, maybe as a way to make up for the hours a week that he smelled like a farmer. I open the bottle, spray one pump into the air, and walk into the mist.

What if I forget this smell?

They say I should move on, not hang on. Remember him, yes, but get on with life. It will be one thing to look at a photograph once in a while, but keeping his scent?

Don't be weird, Lynn.

I place the bottle in the trash.

⊙ ⊙ ⊙

It's another day closer to the move, and I wake up thinking about what I still have to do. Dad will be here the day after next with a U-Haul. Several friends have volunteered to help, so I don't have to worry about that.

What I do have to think about are the two appointments I have in Sioux Falls this afternoon. One is a postnatal follow-up with my gynecologist, and the other is Carlene's one-month checkup with the pediatrician. Bruce would have been with me, of course, but instead, Eileen will come along. She is understandably obsessed with Carlene and has made me promise, several times, that we will visit regularly.

Before I get out of bed, I reach in the headboard drawer and take out the last letter Bruce wrote to me. I'd been visiting my parents when I suspected I was pregnant again. When I called

Bruce to tell him the home pregnancy test was positive, he was excited, but what he couldn't say on the phone, he wrote in a letter:

July 20, 1982

Hi, honey! It seems like I haven't seen you for a week, but it's only been two days. I miss you very much.

So, Lynn, it looks like you're going to get that baby you always wanted. Aren't I just the best husband? I give you whatever you want. I think I overdid it this time! No, I'm excited about having the baby. Well, I'm not going to have it, you are, but you know what I mean. At the same time, it is kind of scary, isn't it? But I'm sure everything will turn out great.

So, honey, do you miss me?

That's as far as I can read.

"Yes, I miss you!" I want to tell him. "How could you even think I couldn't? Nothing has turned out like we thought, and it *is* scary. I don't want to raise her without you, but I guess I have to. Like you always said, one of us has to be the adult."

I put the letter back in its envelope and slam the drawer shut, which startles Carlene, and she starts to cry.

CHAPTER 9

$\mathbf{M}$y feet are in stirrups when my gynecologist asks if I've thought about what type of birth control I want to use.

I peer around my knees.

"My husband's dead."

He stops what he's doing.

"I'm sorry. I heard about that. Please forgive me."

He finishes in silence.

He asks about Carlene as he washes his hands. I tell him she's the center of everyone's attention. He smiles weakly, then shakes my hand, apologizes again, and wishes me luck.

After he leaves, I remove the sheet and look down at my deflated belly. I'm close to my pre-pregnancy weight, although my ideal weight, according to life insurance charts, is at least thirty pounds away.

Since puberty, I've been just overweight enough that every doctor I've met, even when seeing them for nothing more than a sore throat, advises me (or my mother) to watch my weight (which she does).

"Suck it in, Lynnie!" is her ongoing advice.

I roll my fleshy belly between my fingers. The stretchmarks haven't faded much, and now, instead of wrapped tightly around my lower abdomen, they cascade like tributaries on a map.

It was a few days before Halloween when I'd noticed the first one in the bathroom mirror.

"Bruce!"

He came flying through the door. "What? What's wrong?"

"Look." I pointed to a light-purple streak to the right of my belly button. "Is that a stretchmark?"

"You scared the hell out of me!" He bent over to take a look.

"Sorry. I was just really hoping to avoid them. My mom never had them."

He kissed my cheek. "It'll be worth it."

It wasn't stretchmarks I dreaded in pregnancy as much as gaining weight. I didn't share that with Bruce because I knew he wouldn't understand. Whenever he felt "sluggish," the term he used when he gained a pound or two, he cut back on desserts and played a few additional basketball games at the rec center.

But still, Bruce knew I struggled with body acceptance. Many times, he'd listened to me bitch about my wide hips, flat butt, too-long legs, too-short torso, and baby face, and every time I did, he said I was beautiful.

"You're just being nice," I'd say.

"I never lie."

Maybe someday I'll love my body as much as he loved my body, especially my pregnant body, but not today because he's not here to remind me that stretchmarks are beautiful. That I'm beautiful.

⊙ ⊙ ⊙

Unlike the gynecologist, the pediatrician walks in the room prepared. After his initial phone call the day after Bruce died, he has checked in on Carlene and me a few more times.

"Did her eye infection clear up quickly?"

"Yes."

"How is nursing?"

"The warm compresses aren't helping. I'm mostly bottle-feeding now."

"That's okay. As long as she's gaining weight."

Still, I feel guilty. I've let Bruce down.

He examines Carlene and declares her healthy and thriving. I tell him we are moving and ask if he could recommend a pediatrician in the Minneapolis area. He says he has a friend with a practice in Minnetonka and that he'll have the contact information at the front desk when I check out.

Carlene starts to fuss.

"Can I feed her first?"

"Take all the time you need," he says, closing the door behind him.

I hold Carlene at my left breast since the right one has abandoned us. Softly, I start to sing "Children of the Heavenly Father" until I get to the line, "From all evil things he spares them," and I think about how, if that was true, I wouldn't be a widow sitting in a pediatrician's office feeding my daughter the meager offerings of my one working breast.

When I was a child, Dad usually put me to bed. After reading me a story and listening to my prayers, he'd tuck me in and turn out the lights. After he left, I would fold my hands again and whisper another prayer asking that, in the morning, could there please be a princess dress in my closet?

Even when I was five years old, I knew that wasn't how God worked, but I thought, *Why not ask?*

Some people have told me that Bruce's death was God's will or that God needed him in his heavenly choir, neither of which makes sense. What grand theological purpose was served by taking a young man away from his family? I knew God wasn't going to give five-year-old me a princess dress, but he could have stopped that train if he wanted to, or at the very least, made Bruce see it in time. So why didn't he?

I stop singing and stare at Carlene, who is asleep again. I lay her in her seat and adjust my clothing. I have more important things to do right now than wonder about God, and it is not a conversation I can have with my mother-in-law.

I walk out of the room and hand the car seat to Eileen before retrieving the information about our new pediatrician from the receptionist.

Part Two

An Obesity of Grief

It's early June, and I'm awakened by the 5:30 sunrise pouring through my bedroom window. I still get confused some mornings and wake up wondering where I am, even though I've lived in this apartment for five weeks.

Carlene is asleep in her crib in the corner, and Lisa is asleep in the other bedroom. Lisa works as a landscaper at a local golf course and is living with us for the summer until she moves back to Jasper to marry Curt.

I fell asleep last night reading one of Bruce's letters, and his words are still on my mind: "I watched the play *All the Way Home* tonight. It was sad because the lead character got killed and his wife had to adjust to it. It made me think of you. Of how much we care about each other. How much we love each other. I don't want to ever lose that."

I'm still not sure what to do with death, but I would tell Bruce that what I've learned so far is that "adjust" isn't it. Adjust is straightening a tie or leveling a picture on a wall. Death requires that you live with the thousand changes, some as small as atoms, created in its wake. My one working breast gave up a few weeks ago. I sold our remaining grain to the elevator and our pigs to my brother-in-law, although I heard that most of the baby pigs died soon after. The Jasper ambulance service sent me a bill for its response to Bruce's accident, even though there was nothing anyone could do to save him. "Nothing personal," someone wrote on it. But it felt personal. Not in a paranoid way, like they were out to hurt me, but in an exclusionary way. I read the death certificate. I have a pretty good idea what they saw and I didn't:

"brain laceration," "hemorrhage," "skull fractures." That made it personal.

Even though his absence is everywhere, I limit how much of Bruce I allow in, thinking it will make his death easier to live with. I put up one photo from our wedding, but I won't unpack the coffee pot. I sold our two-door red Chevy and bought a four-door silver Oldsmobile. Still, almost every day, there is a new emotional surprise, either something I haven't felt before or didn't think I'd feel again because apparently there is no expiration date on feelings. Like when my brother Matthew brought over photos he had taken when my family came to visit the weekend before Bruce died. In the one that takes my breath away, Bruce is sitting in the rocking chair he'd bought me as an early Mother's Day gift. He's cradling Carlene in the crook of his left arm and looking at her pensively, unaware Matthew is taking a picture. He's wearing work jeans and a red flannel shirt with a red and white raglan underneath. I can smell his earthy, honest scent, feel my fingers through his hat-rough hair, see our daughter's breath rise and fall through her blanket, her eyes drifting into sleep, and then the pain of loss shoots through me, like an assassin's bullet.

Last week, when I brought over another box of things to store in my parents' basement, Dad walked out of the garage with Bruce's winter jacket.

"Where did you get that?" I asked. "I know I put that in the giveaway pile."

"Matthew can wear it this winter."

Unlike when I'm angry with my mother, I could be angry at Dad without fear of repercussions, and I was hurt that—like so many men since Bruce died—he thought he knew better than me about what was best for me.

"Someone else, someone not here, can wear it. I don't want to look at it again!"

"Well, then, I'll put it somewhere."

A few years later, I will find it in the closet of my parents' vacation camper, and I will feel the same way I do now, my feelings and wishes disregarded and dismissed.

Yesterday, our small tax refund arrived, and I brought it to the bank. At the drive-through window, I placed the check in the tube and pressed send. The teller looked at it and said, "I'm sorry, ma'am. Your husband needs to sign this check, too."

"He's dead!" I yelled into the speaker. Why does this truth have to be spoken so often?

She stared at me through the glass, probably grateful it was bulletproof.

"Um, I need to talk to my manager," she said.

"You do that!"

She came back a minute later with a receipt.

"Here you go" was all she said.

I wouldn't have thanked me, either.

⊙ ⊙ ⊙

My father-in-law's change of heart seems genuine. True to his word, Walt has been kind, and not in a forced way. On my first visit, a few weeks after I moved, he and I ran errands. When we stopped for gas, one of his friends pulled up at the pumps.

"Hey, Walt," the man said.

"Hey, have you met my daughter-in-law?" Walt had never introduced me to anyone before, and he certainly never referred to me as his daughter-in-law. "She's Bruce's."

It would seem he left off "wife," but that's how Bruce's family referred to spouses. I used to bristle when I heard others introduced in this passive, possessive way, but to hear Walt introduce me as "Bruce's" was both apt and comforting. I *was* Bruce's, and I would always be Bruce's, and I felt safely tethered to Walt and Eileen in that way.

Bruce is often an awkward silence when I'm with others, though. It's not that people don't care; they just don't know what to say. It's why I love my job pouring tap beer and calling tee times at the nine-hole golf course where Lisa works. It doesn't pay much, but for a few hours a week, I'm not Poor Lynn.

So why am I still drawn to Jasper, where my widowhood is tender and nothing there is mine anymore?

In May, I attended Jasper High School's graduation. Instead of buying hymnals, I used some of the money people put in the sympathy cards to establish two scholarships in Bruce's name. Afterward, I went to a party and ran into Sam. When I lived in Jasper the first time, Sam was one of the few people I knew who didn't live on a farm. He was a couple of years older than me, but the way lives intersect in a small town—I was friends with the sister of his girlfriend, that kind of thing—we knew each other well enough. On weekend trips to Jasper, after my family moved to Plymouth, Sam and I were at some of the same parties, and we would chat, sometimes flirt, but nothing more.

Early in our relationship, Bruce and I went to a party at Sam's house. When the party broke up, Sam pulled me aside while Bruce and the others walked out to their cars. I thought he was going to tell me that I'd left something, but instead, he kissed me and said, "Come back tonight. Stay with me." I didn't go back, but I also didn't tell Bruce. I passed it off as an act of drunken lust, nothing more. Sam remained our friend and was a pallbearer at Bruce's funeral.

At the graduation party, Sam and I were both several beers in when he asked me to go home with him. Carlene was with Walt and Eileen, and they knew I planned to stay overnight with a friend in Jasper. I just didn't imagine that friend would be Sam.

While planning Bruce's funeral, I'd said, perhaps too emphatically, that no, I didn't want to be buried next to Bruce when asked if I wanted one plot or two. It was a fair question, but I was planning *his* funeral; I wasn't ready to plan mine. As soon as the words tumbled out of my mouth, I considered the subtext of the question. Surrounded by Bruce's parents and siblings, I felt like I was also being asked, "How much do you love Bruce? Will you be devoted to him for the rest of your life, or will you forget about him?"

As I lay next to Sam, sore like I lost my virginity, my heart aching and guilty, I asked myself the same questions. How could I love Bruce and sleep with someone else, especially one of his friends?

The next morning, I went to the cemetery. When I drove up to the gate, I was unsure which way to turn. The last time I was there, at the graveside service, my sense of direction had been thrown off by all the snow, the people, the tent, the death.

I got out of my car and walked along the gravel road that wound around the plots. To my left, near a stand of trees, ornate markers loomed supine over those buried a century ago, as if protecting their dead. There were no trees around Bruce's grave that I remembered, so I walked toward the section with more modern headstones. Several yards away, I spotted a plot with sprouts of new grass poking unevenly through the topsoil. As I got closer, I saw a gray granite marker, no bigger than an old Webster's dictionary, tucked in the soil. I sat down and lay my hands on its icy surface. Although the sun was hot on my skin, I had goosebumps. Etched only with Bruce's name and the dates of his birth and death, it hinted at nothing else of his life.

What will people think when they see this?

I know it wasn't a lot of money, but I thought the budget number I'd given the monument company would have stretched further than the sad, near "unknown" quality of the stone beneath my hands.

"I promise that someday, I'll buy you something better," I said, but I was talking into the wind. Bruce wasn't there, not even a little bit. I felt nothing but alone, dead among the dead. I stood up and walked back to my car without saying goodbye.

CHAPTER 11

Lisa and Curt's wedding is in four months, and stupid me ordered my bridesmaid's dress a size smaller because I thought it would give me incentive to lose weight. It did for a few weeks, but too much beer and pizza brought me back to where I am now, the same weight I was before I got pregnant. Bruce wouldn't care, but I suspect other men will. No one has said anything about my body, but I never undress completely when I sleep with someone new. Not that there have been many since Sam, but there have been a few.

I can either get serious about losing weight or have my dress altered. Neither should be an excuse to beg out of the wedding. That's not what I want to do anyway. I love weddings! I was the matron of honor at a friend's wedding in Iowa a few weeks ago, a small affair in a college chapel, and I got through that just fine. It's *where* Curt and Lisa are getting married that makes me dread this particular wedding. I want to believe me when I assure Lisa that I'll be fine, but when I imagine walking down *that* aisle again, my hands begin to shake. I just know I'll think about Bruce and the funeral and how Bruce isn't standing next to Curt in the exact spot Curt stood next to Bruce when we got married, and I'll break down sobbing and embarrass myself, and I'll be Poor Lynn all over again.

I need to get my shit together and stop crying over the dumbest things. Last weekend, when Lisa was in Jasper, my brother Matthew came over with a joint. Carlene was asleep for the night, so we sat on the deck and smoked. Usually pot makes me feel mellow and happy, and it did until we went inside and started watching MTV, and the video for Journey's "Separate Ways" came on. I sang along as tears fell down my face.

"What's wrong?" Matthew asked.

"I . . . I . . . sometimes feel like we were nothing, you know? Like we were just playing house."

Matthew started to cry, too. Having been raised in an atmosphere of potential rejection, we both found solace in Bruce's unwavering acceptance. And with Bruce, Matthew also experienced the kind of familial rapport he'd witnessed between many of his friends and their brothers. Inside jokes and late-night talks with his brother-in-law were more than Matthew would ever have with his own brother.

Right now, I don't know what's crueler—losing something beautiful or never having it at all?

"Why did this have to happen?" he asked.

"I don't know," I said, and we ate from the bowl of peanut M&Ms, crying quietly until the last chord.

I do have genuinely happy moments, and yet I seem to do happy all wrong. Out one night with a couple Bruce and I used to hang out with, the husband said to me while we were dancing, "I think my wife misses your husband more than you do."

Despite all the changes in the last few months, I still want to go to college. Bruce had encouraged me to apply to Augustana College, even though we weren't sure how we'd pay for it, given the emerging farm crisis in 1982. Corn and soybean prices had plummeted and showed no signs of rebounding, and we often talked about what we'd do if we had to quit farming. Bruce said he'd find some kind of job in agriculture, but he also wanted to pursue a music career. I wanted that for him, too. Because nothing felt impossible when we were together, we decided I would go to school part-time and work part-time, and he'd sing whenever and wherever he could.

My parents have a subscription to the *Jasper Journal*, and I read that my former neighbor's son will attend Golden Valley Lutheran College, a small two-year liberal arts college not far from where I live. I decide to apply there, too. I mean, why not? Getting rejected by a college wouldn't be the worst thing to happen this year.

⊙ ⊙ ⊙

Turns out my high school guidance counselor, the one who thought I was better suited for marriage than college, was wrong. I start college the Tuesday after Labor Day.

CHAPTER 12

Last year, on my nineteenth birthday, I bought Bruce a bottle of whiskey because I was finally old enough to legally buy liquor. This year, on my twentieth birthday, I went to a weekend softball tournament in Mankato with one of Bruce's many cousins, one I met for the first time at another cousin's wedding last month. He is several years older than me and looks nothing like Bruce. He is nothing like Bruce at all, actually, except that they share the same last name.

Eileen might know I've been seeing him, or at least she suspects I've been dating again. When I talked to her on the phone recently, she said, with no context, that it's harder to lose a son than a husband. I said that wasn't fair since neither of us have lost both. She said that I can always get remarried, but she couldn't replace her son. I said I could never replace Bruce, that there is no one like him, but I understand her point.

What she doesn't know, what no one knows, is that I miss Bruce so much that I'm afraid I will break apart and die if I don't stay ahead of the pain that exists in the periphery and chases me like a shadow. It's why I'm rarely alone, and if it means I have to invent feelings for someone to throw that shadow off my scent, I'll do it.

⊙ ⊙ ⊙

When I was five years old, I nearly drowned in a neighbor's pool. I remember choking as I slipped under the surface. Through the water, I saw a shimmering outline of someone at the edge of the pool and a hand reaching into the water. I remember my body pulled up and set down smoothly on the concrete. As I coughed violently, someone wrapped a towel around my shoulders.

I feel that same kind of drowning now, only that shimmering outline of someone standing on the edge isn't offering me a hand. I was denied the grant I applied for, the one the college said I was sure to get. Even though I had filed 1982 taxes with my late husband, and would have to again for the 1983 tax year, because of my age, the grant required me to submit my parents' tax returns, too. My parents haven't claimed me on their taxes since 1981, but that didn't matter to the grant gods, and Dad's income, a middle-class wage at best, made me ineligible.

There was one more way I could pay for the year. Before we met, Bruce's family agreed that Bruce would take out a life insurance policy on his mother as the way to buy out his siblings for the farm when she passed. When we were married, Bruce replaced his brother John with me as co-owner of the policy, or at least that's what Bruce directed the insurance agent to do. Because Bruce died, and I didn't want to own the farm, I asked the agent to cash it in. He told me that for optimal return, about $4,000, I should wait to cash it in just before the next payment was due in mid-September. When I called the agent on the date we agreed to, he told me he was sorry, but John had already cashed it in.

"But how? I own that policy."

No, explained the agent. I was the sole beneficiary.

"But that wasn't the point of the policy! You were supposed to make me co-owner."

It was all there in the paperwork, he said. John remained co-owner while I was the beneficiary. Bruce obviously hadn't read the fine print.

I called John. "You cashed in the life insurance? I assume you're sending me a check?"

"No," he said, adding that Bruce would have wanted him to use the money to take care of the farm.

Did he know his brother at all?

I'd wrapped the phone cord so tightly around my wrist that my fingers were cold.

"Bruce paid over $15,000 into that policy! He would have wanted to take care of his wife and child!"

My argument got me nowhere, and my next phone call was to a lawyer. I sued John and the insurance agent, but the lawyer said that any settlement would come too late to pay for college, and I had to drop out.

I now work in the mailroom at Musicland's corporate headquarters. Benefits include decent health insurance, and I met Sammy Hagar and The Go-Go's when they came in for a tour. I've made a few friends, and we go out after work sometimes, but it doesn't seem to matter where I go or who I'm with, nearly everything I do, every breath I take, is weighed down by a boulder of grief. I thought by now that enough time had passed to dilute Bruce's memory to a palatable level, but I'm starting to think maybe David was right, that time doesn't heal a damn thing.

CHAPTER 13

Wooden *pews are uncomfortable even when you're not pregnant,* I think as I shift in my seat at the back of the church, the same place I sat on Sunday mornings the last few months I was pregnant so I could leave without disturbing anyone when I needed to get up and stretch my back.

When I told Lisa in October that I couldn't be in the wedding, she'd hugged me and said, "Oh, my gosh, Lynn, don't worry about it!" which made me cry even harder.

"God, all I've done this year is let people down!"

"Don't be silly," she said. "You haven't let me down! I understand."

Peering down the aisle, I see a basket of fall flowers placed near the steps where Curt and his groomsmen would stand. They are there in memory of Bruce, but they seem out of place, sequestered from the larger bouquets on the altar, the organ, and the piano.

The soloists begin singing "The Wedding Song" as Curt takes his place near the basket of flowers. I wonder if he's thinking about his best friend and struggling with the dichotomy of loss and love like I am.

When the song is finished, the organist begins to play, and the processional begins. The flower girls start down the aisle, giggling as they throw petals. The bridesmaids, with their brilliant smiles and beautiful hair and bouquets, walk past me, and I'm crushed by jealousy. I should be walking down that aisle, too, and stealing glances at my handsome husband standing next to Curt. Instead, I am as lonely as that basket of flowers, lost in a familiar place; my sorrow is an intruder, out of sync with the joy in the air.

The congregation stands as Lisa and her father begin their walk down the aisle. I swallow the lump in my throat and smile as she walks past. I'm happy for her, I truly am, but I'm sad for me. So sad that, when the procession ends, I do the only thing I know how to do. I leave.

CHAPTER 14

The day after Musicland's Christmas party, I wake up, hungover, next to a marketing exec. I try to recall the details that got me here, in his house, in his bed, and I draw a blank. I'm not even sure where I am. I sit up a little and see Medicine Lake through the patio door, so I'm not too far from home.

A few minutes later, he wakes up, hungover, and he looks at me with abject disbelief. Fuck him. Like screwing the girl from the mailroom is the worst thing he's done in his life.

Without a word, we get dressed. As he drives me to my car that I remember I left in the hotel parking lot, I think about how, at work on Monday, as I push the mail cart through the marketing department, he won't look up from whatever he is reading when I drop his mail in the in-box on his desk, and how I will find the guy from the warehouse, someone more my type, and tell him I've changed my mind; I will go out with him.

◉ ◉ ◉

It's Christmas Eve. Carlene and I will soon go to my sister Emily's Christmas program at church and, afterward, to my parents' house to open gifts. I dress Carlene in a lacy lavender dress, white tights, and a sweater before setting her on the floor with a bottle half-filled with watered-down apple juice. She crawls, bottle swinging from her mouth, over to the Christmas tree. She sits, grabs her bottle with both hands, and stares at the lights as she drinks. I want to capture the moment, but I have to be sneaky. Photos of Carlene in action are nearly impossible to take because, whenever she sees a camera, she stops what she's doing and poses with a wide, toothless grin and claps her hands.

Quietly, without her suspecting, I take her picture.

A few weeks ago, Carlene started "talking." She taps my face with her hands and says, "Mum mum mum," which makes me both proud and petrified. When I try to get her to say, "Da da," she always looks confused.

"Who's da da?" I imagine she asks.

"He's the guy we're both growing up without," I tell her.

I put on Dan Fogelberg's album, *The Innocent Age*, a Christmas gift from Bruce in 1981. Listening to music is one ritual from our life that I continue. We listened to music every time we got ready to go out, when we ate dinner, or played games on a winter night. We listened to music in the car, and I know he listened to music in the tractor. Before I realize it, I'm daydreaming about what might have happened in the moments before the train struck his tractor, and I wonder what song he was singing.

Music is the only safe place I feel him. A song is ambiguous, subjected only to the memory in my mind, unlike a photograph that is concrete in its detail, stark in its reminder of what is gone. Listening to a familiar song, I can feel us dancing or making love. Music also articulates things I seem unable to. Bonnie Tyler singing about falling in love and falling apart makes me feel less alone.

I often sing to Carlene. One of my favorites is a song my mother used to sing to me: "I love you, a bushel and a peck, a bushel and a peck and a hug around the neck . . ." I tickle Carlene's belly and kiss her plump cheeks. She laughs and I usually laugh, too, although sometimes I start to cry, but she just thinks her mama is being silly. I hope it's always that way, that she never knows how hard everything is right now.

CHAPTER 15

May 1984

I'm pregnant, and because I'm further along than I realized, the father can't be who I thought it was.

After Christmas, I started to think I had no future in Minnesota and considered moving far away, maybe to California, somewhere I could start over and escape the winter and the damned grief. January has always been a difficult month for me, even when Bruce was around. Everything feels heavy, from my body zipped up in a coat to the snow piled on my car. Instead of moving, though, I decided I would become a paramedic, my career choice when I was ten years old. The first step was to enroll in a twelve-week advanced first aid class at the American Red Cross. There, I met two men who changed my future more than California ever could.

Lee was the class instructor. He was handsome in a Mr. Rogers kind of way, only without the warm smile or cardigan. He was a Green Beret in Vietnam and has several black belts in karate, which might explain why he's emotionally cold and demands our bandages and slings are applied perfectly. After class one night, as he sat at a table grading tests, I stood in front of him, waiting to ask him a question. Before I could say anything, he looked up, his face expressionless, and said, "Will you have dinner with me on Tuesday?"

"I, uh . . ." *Is he supposed to ask a student for a date?* "I . . . yeah . . . sure."

I wrote down my phone number on an index card.

"I'll call you tomorrow," he said and went back to grading tests.

I didn't mention that I had a kid, and when he picked me up Tuesday evening, I had eleven-month-old Carlene on my hip.

"She's beautiful," he said, exuding a gentleness that no one in class would suspect he possessed.

"Yeah, I like her," I said and kissed her cheek.

He handed me a bright-red tropical flower. An anthurium, he called it, from Hawaii, where he was born and raised. I'd never seen such an exotic flower, not in Minnesota in February, and especially not one so boldly sexual.

For two months, Lee fussed over Carlene and me, but he was prone to pouting, and he subtly put me down if he didn't get his way. Twice my age, the generation between us often caused him to behave more like a father than a lover, and I grew increasingly frustrated with his skewed perception of me, like how he always called me Pretty Green Eyes even though my eyes are blue. Lee saw what he wanted to see, and I couldn't change that. By the time I learned I was pregnant, I'd been dating RJ, a fellow classmate, for three weeks. When I told RJ about the baby, he said it didn't matter that it wasn't his; he would be its father.

CHAPTER 16

Cassandre Louise is the largest baby in the neonatal intensive care unit. At just over eight pounds, she fills the small Isolette meant for preemies.

"Come on, baby, breathe," I'd heard the doctor say in the seconds after she was born, and it felt like a lifetime before Cassie let out her first cry. Although her APGAR score roared to a nine at the five-minute check, she was taken to the NICU.

"Just a precaution," the pediatrician assured me.

RJ and I look through the window of the NICU and see Cassie swaddled in a white, blue, and pink striped blanket. Her eyes are wide open, and she's looking around like she woke up on a stranger's couch. *She's definitely my daughter*, I think, although, she almost wasn't.

I liked RJ enough; he was smart and had a sarcastic sense of humor, but he was also stubborn and cocky and often angry, and I wasn't sure I wanted to raise my children with him. Lee said he would help me any way I let him, so when I told him I might need him to sign adoption papers, he said he would. At the time, giving the baby to someone else to raise seemed the only way to fix the mess I'd made.

Then I told my mother, and her response went something like this: "How could you let this happen? You're just like your father. You think sex is so important! You can't take care of another baby! You think it will be easy to give up a baby? Who am I going to talk to about this? I certainly can't talk to your father. And don't you say anything to him! I'll take care of it! No one thinks about me and what I go through! Do you think my life is easy? You have no idea . . ."

I didn't bother telling her the best part, that RJ wasn't the father.

At twenty years old, I hadn't yet learned how to extract my mother when she inserted herself into my personal life, but I should have known not to expect her support and advice, not after all the times I'd witnessed similar angry behavior toward my siblings when they did something that let her down. Like it or not, my pregnancy had become about her, and it was up to me to make things right.

As usual, Mom didn't speak to me for a week, and as usual, I spent the week agonizing over what to do to make her talk to me again. I eventually decided to keep the baby and raise it with RJ, but I had no idea if that was the decision she wanted me to make since, when I told her, she didn't say a word.

At five months, my blood pressure spiked, just like when I was pregnant with Carlene. While I didn't have preeclampsia, my doctor still wanted me to stay off my feet as much as I could, which made walking a mail cart around a large building every day no longer feasible. I found a part-time job as a receptionist at a real estate agency, but without a full-time paycheck, I didn't make enough money to afford the apartment anymore. I asked my parents if Carlene and I could move in with them for a few months. Mom was still angry, but she adored Carlene, and she agreed to let us live there.

I saw RJ almost every day, although he often seemed encased in a bubble that no one could penetrate. He only had one friend that I knew of, and even though he was an only child, he wasn't close to his parents. Bruce used to tell me everything. I knew how he felt about me and about us every minute of every day. RJ was a riddle, and often silent and cold. I struggled to feel what I thought I should feel for someone willing to be the father of a baby that wasn't his, yet something nagged at me every time I thought about raising my kids with him. One evening, RJ came to see me at work, and when he walked in the door, that nagging feeling ran up my spine, and I spoke from that feeling.

"I think we should break up," I said.

"Oh . . . kay . . . why?"

"We just . . ." *How do you tell someone that they make you uncomfortable without hurting their feelings?* "I . . . just think it's best."

He rapped his knuckles a few times on the counter, nodded, and walked out the door.

For the first time in months, I relaxed.

RJ's car was in the driveway when I got home. Mom met me at the door.

"What do you think you're doing?" she hissed. "RJ's in the living room, crying. How could you do this? Do you think you're going to raise that baby *and* Carlene by yourself?"

Even if she knew the truth, that RJ wasn't the father, she'd have argued that RJ was willing to take on the responsibility of not only *two* children that weren't his but a crazy woman as well.

"Where's Carlene?" I asked.

"She's in bed. Now go in there and talk to him!"

RJ paced as I sat down on the couch.

"I love you, and you want to throw it away?" he yelled, his face inches from mine. "Bitch!"

Mom, who'd obviously heard him, stomped in the room and yelled, "Don't you talk to her like that!"

RJ slowly turned around and walked over to her. He stood over Mom's slight five-foot-three-inch frame, his eyes pinched in anger. He raised his hand and leaned into her like he was going to slap her.

"Go ahead!" she challenged him. "Be a big man!"

He hesitated. They stared at each other, frozen in place like statues.

My heart was beating a million miles a minute, and the baby was turning circles in my belly. *This man is going to hit my mother! Where is Dad?*

I stood up and screamed, "Stop it! Just stop it!"

I plopped back down on the couch and started to cry.

Then I felt a cramp.

"Oh, no," I whispered. I was only six months along, too soon to be in labor. The cramp got stronger, and I didn't feel the baby moving anymore. "I need to go to the hospital."

Mom and RJ's statue pose collapsed, and both turned off their anger as quickly as it turned on.

Mom helped me off the couch and to the car, where RJ had already opened the door for me.

"Everything will be fine," they said.

I remembered Bruce said something similar in the car on our way to the Pipestone hospital before the miscarriage. I didn't believe Bruce then, and I didn't believe them now.

My doctor was on call and met us at the hospital. I was hooked up to a fetal monitor, and we were all relieved to hear a strong heartbeat. After an exam, she said the baby was fine and that I'd experienced Braxton-Hicks contractions.

"But," she said, "your blood pressure is worrisome. No stress for the next three months."

She instructed me to keep my feet elevated for most of the day and sleep on my left side at night. I could still work a few hours a week since I sat for most of my shift, but she said I shouldn't pick up Carlene anymore.

"Let someone hand her to you," she said, not realizing how complicated her instructions would be.

On the way home, RJ said he was sorry and that he still wanted us to be a family. I needed too much help to say no.

In October, two months before my due date, RJ, Carlene, and I moved into a two-bedroom, roach-infested apartment. The roaches were exterminated, but the nagging feeling at the back of my neck remained.

⊙ ⊙ ⊙

Cassie is now in the regular nursery and has no apparent lung issues. RJ left a few minutes ago to pick up Carlene from Mom and Dad's. He will bring her by tomorrow to meet her sister.

I'm tired but high on adrenaline, so I start a letter to Walt and Eileen.

Even though they've been nothing but wonderful to Carlene and me, given our history of poor communication during times of conflict, I didn't tell them I was pregnant the last time I saw them, which was just before I started to show. They saw Carlene for a weekend last month, thanks to my dad who, sworn to secrecy, drove her to and from what has become our regular meeting place halfway between their home and mine. Carlene, not yet two years old, had no idea I was having a baby, so I knew she wouldn't tell them.

I try to explain without too much detail (they bristle at detail) how Cassie came to be, stating simply that since Bruce died, I haven't made the best decisions. I finish with "I love you," which is true, and a promise to send a photo of Carlene with her baby sister. I place the letter in my suitcase and plan to mail it when I go home in a few days.

I take out my journal and settle back in bed to write.

On my eleventh birthday, someone gave me a small, blue faux leather diary, and I wrote in it faithfully. During high school,

I filled four notebooks with doodles and song lyrics, teenage questions, and teenage insights. When Bruce and I got engaged, in an impassioned gesture, I decided to burn them, as if by burning the past, I was showing Bruce my commitment to our future.

"Are you sure you want to do this?" he asked, just before I threw them in the fire.

"Yes," I said. "Nothing before you matters."

I know now, at twenty-one, that my life before Bruce mattered, but who knows why we do what we do when we're eighteen?

I haven't journaled since the day I burned those notebooks, although lately, I've written some thoughts on scraps of paper that I keep in my nightstand. A few weeks ago, RJ surprised me with a crimson leatherbound journal. He said he found my scraps of paper and thought I might like to keep my writing in one place. I was grateful for his gift, but wondered, *What was he looking for in my nightstand?*

I open the journal and read my first entry: "In a few days, I'm going to have a baby. I really hope things go well. I've been so paranoid since Bruce died that someone else I love will die, too.

"I also want to be loved. No, wait, I am loved. I want to be 'in love' again. I think I love RJ, but he's so damn frustrating sometimes. Bruce was so uncomplicated."

The door opens, and four people wheel in a woman on a gurney and move her onto the other bed.

"Hello," she says, her voice groggy.

"Hello," I say.

"She'll probably sleep all night," a nurse says and closes the curtain between us.

In a few minutes, the staff leave, and judging by the woman's gentle, even breathing, I assume she's asleep. I return to my journal and write: "I love my life, my family, my home, but I wish

Bruce was here to share all of this with me. I'm being so unfair to RJ, though. We have a lot together, right? When am I going to realize that? I just have to give myself more time.

"Toto played on the radio a few minutes ago, and it reminded me of the New Year's party at Sam's when I was pregnant with Carlene. The cigarette smoke and warm air made me sick. Curt and Lisa were leaving, so they took me home. Bruce came home just before midnight, and we brought in 1983 in bed, of course. God, we were so good together. It was tough losing my best friend. I haven't spoken with anyone quite the same."

A nurse backs into the room, pulling a bassinet. Cassie is squirming and squeaking.

"Would you like to feed your baby?" she whispers.

"Yes, I would." I set my journal on the table and sit upright.

She hands me Cassie, and I measure the heft of her in my arms. Cassie feels tiny compared to Carlene, who was born two inches longer and a pound heavier.

"Hello, little girl," I whisper and kiss her forehead. Cassie is on the verge of a full-blown scream, and I rock her softly. "Shhh, shhh . . ."

The nurse hands me a bottle, and a pang of guilt hits my heart. I know I should breastfeed, but given my experience the last time, I don't have the confidence to try again.

"I'll be back in a little bit," the nurse says.

Cassie falls asleep after a few ounces. I burp her and then lay her on the bed to change her diaper. *There's no doubt who her father is,* I think as I take in her short legs and long face.

I'd called Lee this morning before RJ got here to tell him today was the day.

"It didn't have to be this way, you know," he said. "I would have married you."

"But I don't love you" seemed an inappropriate reply, so I said nothing.

"Well, good luck," he said and hung up.

I pick up Cassie and hold her close.

"We're gonna be alright," I whisper in her ear before falling asleep, too.

CHAPTER 17

Journal entry, August 1985

"I try to be nice, understanding, but RJ brushes me off,
ignores me. He won't let me get close to him at all."

Yet, in a few hours, I'm going to marry him.

RJ and I were required to attend three premarital counseling sessions before the pastor of our church would agree to marry us. During our first meeting, he gave us a compatibility quiz. I answered the questions honestly, and as far as I know, so did RJ. We scored below fifty percent, which made us nervous, but the pastor assured us that the quiz didn't mean much. It was just a place to start the conversation about what we would each bring to our marriage. As long as we had God in our lives, he said, our marriage would be strong.

RJ is new to religion and was recently baptized. He said he did it for the girls and me, but I suspect his conversion was more rebellion than an act of faith. His parents are atheists and oppose organized religion. His becoming a Christian was a big "fuck them," and honestly, how much of a role God will play in our marriage, I can't say. Going to church is more of a social event than worship, plus it makes my parents happy. So does marrying RJ. The girls need a legal father, they said, and so I will give them a legal father.

My parents live a few blocks from the church, so I'm getting ready at their house. I just returned from the appointment I made with a hair stylist I picked out of the Yellow Pages. She fixed my hair in a French braid like I asked her to, but staring at my face in the bathroom mirror, I wonder if a braid was the best choice this time.

The day I married Bruce, his sister-in-law had painstakingly braided my hair into ten narrow rows and gathered them in a bun where she attached my veil. It was a stunning style, and I couldn't believe it was me when she was done.

I take a sip of wine and consider my face—plump and flushed—and how it reflects everything that happened this year.

At my six-week postpartum checkup, I'd told my doctor that I wanted my tubes tied, but she said I was carrying too much fat in my lower stomach.

"Come back when you've lost some weight," she said and offered no suggestions on how to do that. For two weeks, I subsisted on puffed wheat, milk, oranges, SlimFast, cheese popcorn, and Blatz Light before I gave up, having lost nothing. Since then, I've gained an additional twenty pounds.

I pour another glass of wine and dot foundation on my cheeks. I hum the song playing in my head until I realize that it's "Forever Autumn," which always reminds me of Bruce. I'll never find another Bruce, but I've trapped myself in a discomforting relationship, and I'm too afraid to let it go. Too afraid there's no one other than RJ who will ever want me. I finish putting on makeup and take one last look. "Good enough."

In what used to be my bedroom, I pull on a silk pink dress with puffy sleeves that is more appropriate for a bridesmaid than a bride. The fabric clings to my stomach before relaxing and flowing over my hips.

"You'd better get your ass down that aisle before he changes his mind," I say, smoothing the fabric.

◉ ◉ ◉

Both of my grandmothers traveled from Jasper (separately, of course) to be at my wedding. Signe and Katinka have never liked each other, or maybe it's more accurate to say that Katinka doesn't like Signe and Signe doesn't care. As Signe mixes easily with people before the service, Katinka sits in the front row, frowning, her arms crossed in her ample lap. I know her well enough to not ask her what's wrong because so few things are ever right in her world, including my body size, and I'm not interested in her assessment of my weight today.

I insisted we not hire a professional photographer, claiming it was too expensive, when the truth is that I can't bear the thought of looking through proofs. People insist on taking photos, though, so RJ and I stand near the altar with the girls—two-and-a-half year old Carlene in front of us and Cassie, eight months, perched on RJ's hip—as our parents and others take turns standing with us in subsequent photos.

"We'll make sure you get copies," a few of them say, and I thank them, knowing I will probably not look at them.

Finally, the "I dos" are over, and we return to Mom and Dad's. After we open gifts, I sneak out to the garage to smoke a joint with my childhood friend, Jeff.

"You sure about this?" he asks. His question isn't about getting high. Jeff is no fan of RJ's, and he's mentioned a few times in the last few months that I seem unhappy.

I inhale and shake my head. "Absolutely!" I say, exhaling. "Things will be great!"

Jeff rolls his eyes. He knows I'm kidding, but he doesn't press me because he knows it won't do any good. Marrying RJ absolves me of widowhood, and while our relationship is often precarious, its fragility distracts me from grief, and for that, I am grateful.

CHAPTER 18

July 1987

The first panic attack was three weeks ago, the night of Dad's heart attack, when I was with my mom and sister Debbie in the hospital waiting room, watching Mickey Mouse cartoons. I was reclined sideways in a chair with my legs dangling over the arm when my stomach started to churn. The feeling crept upward to my heart, which began beating wildly. Then it went to my lungs, and I couldn't complete a full breath. It finally settled in my mind, and I thought, *I'm dying!* Within a few minutes, I was on a gurney in the emergency room, and a doctor was handing me a pill.

"You had a panic attack," he said. "Here, put this under your tongue."

It was Halcion. Valium with a kick, he called it. Within seconds, I was calm. So calm, I forgot why I was at the hospital. Debbie reminded me as she poured me into the front seat of my car to take me home.

"Will Dad be okay?" I asked.

"Probably," she replied just before I fell asleep.

Debbie dropped me off at home, and I staggered into the house. I said hi to RJ and the girls before collapsing in bed. When I woke up two hours later, I felt like I was coming out of anesthesia. When the effects wore off, the same cycle of panic started again.

They gave me ten Halcion when I left the hospital, and I took them all within five days. Panic continued to pour over me like a tsunami. I went to every emergency room in the Minneapolis area, begging for relief, usually in the middle of the night, waking RJ and dragging the kids out of bed because I didn't trust myself to drive. The last ER doctor said I needed to see a psychiatrist and refused to write a script.

"You think this is all in my head?" I asked.

"I don't know," he said. "But drugs aren't the answer."

The next day, I went through the Yellow Pages and, after several calls, found a psychiatrist who advertised a Christian-based practice. The Christian part didn't matter to me; he was the only one who could see me right away.

He was tall and thin and wore a light-gray suit that matched his hair. Instead of giving me Halcion, he assured me I could control my panic through deep breathing and gave me a copy of Herbert Benson's *The Relaxation Response.*

"Come back next week," he said.

Today, my Selectric II typewriter ribbon broke at work, and I began to cry. I cried while I changed it, cried as I typed a memo, and cried when my boss sent me home because I couldn't stop crying. I cried driving home, cried while I made and ate a grilled cheese sandwich, and cried as I dialed the phone to tell the psychiatrist I was crying. I cried even harder when he told me he was checking me into the hospital. A special hospital.

An hour later, RJ drops me off at Golden Valley Health Center. I've stopped crying, but my head feels as dense as a bowling ball.

I fill out insurance forms, and a nurse leads me to a scale in the hallway. I am wearing knee-length knit shorts and a size XXL T-shirt stained at the hem. Tears have washed away my makeup, and my hair is matted to my head. I take off my slip-on canvas shoes with the hole in the toe and lay them beside the scale. The nurse optimistically starts the large metal weight at the 150-pound position and nudges the smaller weight higher. The balance arrow doesn't budge. She moves the large weight to 200 and again moves the small weight higher. The arrow bounces a little around 240. For accuracy, she should move the large weight to 250, but she says cheerfully, "We'll call you two-forty-nine."

I follow her to the room where I will sleep and shower. It is stark and sterile with two crisply made single beds and dull-blue flecked linoleum flooring, but there is a large window that overlooks a lush yard with big trees and benches scattered around.

"Do I have a roommate?" I ask.

"Not at the moment," she says.

I set my bag on the bed nearest the door, even though the bed near the window is more appealing. If I get a roommate, I don't want her to think I'm selfish.

"Meals are in the dining room," the nurse says. "You'll find the group therapy schedule posted in the hall. There are no more today, so try to rest. Dinner is at 5:30."

I call RJ to tell him my room number and let him know he is allowed to visit in the evenings if he wants to.

"Do you want to talk to the girls?" he asks.

I am too upset to be Fake Mommy. "I'll talk to them tomorrow. Give them big hugs from me, though. Tell them I love them."

We hang up and I start to unpack. I remembered to grab my journal, and once my clothes are in the dresser, I sit on the bed and start writing.

Day two, I spend hours in group therapy, feeling completely out of place and ridiculously selfish among people facing electric shock therapy. One woman is the only survivor of a car crash that killed her niece and sister. She was the driver. A chain-smoking young man had locked himself in a closed garage a few weeks ago and started his car's engine. He'd been repeatedly molested as a child.

Can I be a bigger baby? I think as I write my name with a blue crayon on a piece of yellow construction paper. We are drawing a "family tree of feelings." The only thing I feel is guilty for taking up space in a facility meant for people with real problems. I shouldn't have called the psychiatrist. So I'd cried for a few hours? Big deal. People cry.

They make me take a psychological test that asks me to answer yes or no to statements such as, "I would like to do the work of a choir director" and "If I could sneak into the county fair or an amusement park without paying, I would." *Are they kidding me?*

Day three, a psychiatrist comes to my room to go over my test results. She shows me a line chart indicating how I scored in regard to various emotions and behaviors. The line is flowing along nicely, indicating I am "normal" here and "normal" there, just as I expected. Then a steep, jagged line rises across the paper like the Matterhorn. It goes all the way to the top of the chart before plummeting back to the middle.

"That's your anger line," she says.

"What?" I start to laugh. "Just because I don't want to be a choir director, I'm angry? I have nothing to be angry about!"

I explain that I have a panic disorder and that a few days ago, I couldn't stop crying. I just need to calm down. She nods, writes a few notes, and gives me Xanax, which she instructs me to take three times a day. It works almost instantly, but the relentless weeks-long waves of panic have made me afraid of fear.

Day four, a nurse comes to my room to tell me I'm getting a roommate, so while I'm alone, I write in my journal: "I've spent most of my adult life afraid of something. Loss, mostly. Bruce died and my dad nearly died. RJ hasn't said anything about it, but all of this panic has to be a burden on him. I found out today that I lost my job, and we were barely making ends meet in the first place. I wouldn't blame RJ if he left. My girls . . . Jesus, my kids have to be wondering where I am. I have to feel normal again. The Xanax is a good start, but something has to change. I have to change."

Day five, I was allowed to go home after I signed a paper saying

I would visit my psychiatrist weekly. Seriously, though, he's no help. He read the hospital psychiatrist's report and ran with her whole "anger" diagnosis, so I've nicknamed him Dr. Angry.

⊙ ⊙ ⊙

In today's session, Dr. Angry focuses on Bruce. He says it's natural to feel anger toward someone who has died. I don't like where this is going.

"He didn't mean to die," I snap.

I know this is true because a few months after Bruce died, I'd contacted the last person to see him alive, the Burlington Northern engineer. I'd been sick with worry thinking about what happened in those moments before the train struck Bruce's tractor, and I needed to know: Did Bruce realize, at the last second, that the train was going to hit him? Or, the uglier option—the one that haunted me, the one that seemed improbable, impossible, but still, I had to know—did he see the train coming and cross the tracks deliberately?

When the man answered the phone and I identified myself, he became defensive.

"You can't sue me!"

"I promise you, that's not why I called," I assured him. "I need to know, at any point, did my husband see the train?"

The man hesitated. Finally, he said, "The man driving the tractor was looking over his left shoulder the whole time."

The train had approached from Bruce's right.

"I blew the whistle over and over," he continued, his voice tight and constrained. It was as difficult for him to say as it was for me to hear. "But I couldn't get his attention and I couldn't stop."

My heart broke for him, to know a man was going to die and he couldn't do anything to stop it.

"I'm very sorry," I said. "Thank you for telling me."

"Never call me again," he said and hung up.

Dr. Angry leans forward in his chair. "What I mean is, because of your husband's mistake, he left you and a small child. That's a lot to bear. I would be surprised if you weren't angry about that at some point."

It is the first time anyone has suggested that Bruce was culpable for his death. Most blamed fate or said it was God's will. Me? I've blamed Bruce thousands of times.

The world fascinated Bruce, and the smallest things would catch his attention and distract him, especially when he was driving. Once, on our way to a doctor's appointment, when I was too pregnant to drive, we were making our way down a busy street in Sioux Falls. Something out the driver's window—I don't remember what—made Bruce exclaim, "Hey, look at that!"

A split second later, I yelled, "Watch out!"

Thankfully, he didn't rear-end the car ahead of us, but I was pissed.

"Damn it, Bruce! You do this all the time!" I said, recalling the myriad of other near accidents we'd been in.

"I'm sorry!" he said, and I knew he was, and I felt terrible for yelling at him. I feel the same kind of terrible when I get angry and blame him for dying because I know he'd be sorry for that, too.

Talking about this with someone who didn't know Bruce, who doesn't understand how wonderful he was, feels like a betrayal. Bruce isn't here to defend himself. That became my job the day he died.

"Well," I say, "there's nothing anyone can do. I mean, he's dead. Doesn't make sense to blame anyone."

Dr. Angry presses on with his next theory. "Unresolved grief can manifest itself as anger, too. Do you feel like you've adequately mourned his death?"

What does that even mean? Of course, I've mourned him! But I have a life to live, two small children to raise, a marriage to keep together . . .

"Yes, I do," I say.

He takes out a copy of C.S. Lewis's *A Grief Observed* and starts reading. "'No one ever told me that grief felt so like fear.' Do you think the panic attacks could have anything to do with grief?"

"Bruce died four years ago," I reply, tiring of his questions. "And when he did, I cried and I grieved, but I had to move on! I miss him sometimes, sure, but right now, what I'm afraid of is having another panic attack!"

He hands me the book. "Read it. You might find it helpful."

I put it in my purse to be polite.

⊙ ⊙ ⊙

At our next session, Dr. Angry starts by asking about my father's health, which catches me off guard since he usually goes straight to the anger question. I say he's home and recovering well.

Then he asks about RJ.

"Do you have any reason to be angry with him?"

And we're back in the ring.

"All marriages have issues, right?" I say, my defenses on high alert.

I don't tell him that RJ sometimes gets mad at me for reasons too small to remember, and that once in a while, he raises his hand in front of my face in a Ralph Kramden "Why I oughta . . ." kind of way, which scares me a little. I also won't tell him about the actual violence.

It started last summer, after RJ came home from work. I heard him pacing in our bedroom.

"Do you want to grill pork chops for dinner?" I called down the hallway.

"No!" he yelled, and I thought I heard him pound the wall.

I was in the kitchen with Cassie, who was bouncing in her yellow high chair attached to the table, banging her little metal spoon on her bowl and singing. Carlene was visiting Walt and Eileen for the week, and my brother, Matthew, who lived with us, wasn't home from work.

I called down the hall again. "What's wrong?" and this time I was sure he'd punched a hole in the wall. I was afraid my face would be next, or worse, the baby's, so I grabbed Cassie and my purse and ran to my car. As I drove away, he screamed out the front door, "You fucking bitch!" and I remember thinking, *Thank God he didn't call me fat. What would the neighbors think?*

Matthew, Cassie, and I stayed with my parents that night. After Cassie was asleep, Dad poured me a Scotch, and the four of us sat around the dining room table wondering what happened.

"Any idea why he was so mad?" Matthew asked.

"I don't know. Something must have happened at work," I said. My hands were still shaking as I lifted the glass to my lips. "You know he doesn't like to talk about stuff. He came in the house and went straight to the bedroom."

"Well, just be careful, Lynnie. You, too, Matthew," Mom said. "I don't trust him."

I would never tell her that learning to dance around her fluctuating emotions had trained me to dance around RJ's. The steps are complicated: stay quiet, stay small, don't ask questions, and for God's sake, don't make them angrier.

"I don't think he'd ever hurt me," I said, not yet aware that his verbal attacks and noncontact violence were considered abusive just as much as if he'd hit me.

The next morning, I drove past the place where RJ worked. I wanted to be sure he wasn't at home when I returned to inspect the damage. His car was in the parking lot, so I felt safe going home.

As I walked around my house that had been raped by anger, I found a three-inch stab mark through the front door, which I guessed was from the butcher knife RJ had threatened Matthew with when he got home from work. RJ had also put his fist through the inside pane of the front window.

The same numbness I felt when I learned Bruce died covered me. Violence didn't fit my concept of reality. Holes in walls and stab marks in doors were beyond my comprehension. I was a wife and mother. I lived in the suburbs. I had HBO and Showtime. I had a car payment and a job. I went "up north" on summer weekends like a lot of people from Minneapolis.

I put on the radio and began sweeping up the glass. I thought about leaving RJ, but I couldn't afford to live with the kids on my own, and my car was in RJ's name. Besides, I didn't know who I was without RJ. I didn't love him the way I loved Bruce, but I needed him.

RJ called while I was cleaning.

"I'm sorry," he said. "It won't happen again."

He didn't offer an explanation, and I didn't ask for one, afraid that he'd say it was something I'd done, and I didn't want to provoke him.

"Okay," I said. "I'll see you tonight."

After we hung up, I moved the knives from the storage block on the counter to the silverware drawer, just in case, and hung pictures over the holes in the bedroom. A week later, our landlord replaced the window after I told him one of the kids had accidently thrown a ball through it. I couldn't do anything about the stab mark in the door, but we rarely used that entrance anyway, so I didn't notice it again until RJ tried to push me out of the house a few months later.

It was the Saturday before Christmas. The kids were asleep, and RJ was watching TV. He'd been eerily quiet that day, and it was the eerie silence that always scared me the most. I thought it would be best if the kids and I left for a while.

I sat down a few feet away from him. His legs were stretched out across the ottoman, his arms folded at his chest. He held a beer in his right hand. His once warm blue eyes were cold as he stared straight ahead at the television.

"I'm going to take the kids and stay with my parents for a few days."

He turned his head slowly and gave me "the look."

I stood up and went to the kitchen to call my mom. When she answered, I asked if the kids and I could spend the night. Before she could answer, RJ came up behind me and ripped the phone off the wall.

"You're not taking my kids anywhere," he said through a clenched jaw. He grabbed me by my shirt and dragged me to the front door as the phone in the basement began to ring.

It snowed that day, but being out in the cold didn't worry me. I couldn't let him lock me out of the house with the girls inside.

"I'm not leaving without them," I said coolly. I wrestled out of his grip and ran toward the hallway. He ran after me and dragged me back to the front door. Again, I got away. He caught me and pinned me against the kitchen wall. We stared at each other for what felt like an hour.

A knock on the side door stopped whatever was coming next.

"Lynnie, it's Dad." He spoke in the sing-songy voice he used when he read me books as a child. "I brought along a few friends. Can you open the door?"

RJ loosened his grip and yelled at them to go away, that

this was his house. I slipped away and ran down the hallway to Cassie's room. I grabbed her out of her crib and fled to Carlene's room, where I practically threw them into the closet. I popped a Raffi tape into Carlene's tape recorder, hit play, and cranked up the volume just before the police broke through the kitchen door.

The girls thought I was playing a game as I sang the songs in my goofy Mom voice. The floor shook for a few minutes, and then there was silence.

Dad knocked on the bedroom door.

"Lynnie, you can come out now."

He stayed in the room with the girls while I went to talk to the police. In the kitchen, the linoleum was streaked with black scuff marks. The refrigerator was turned almost forty-five degrees.

"I want to press charges," I said to the officer, who was writing something in a notebook.

"No need, ma'am," he said. "Your husband injured a police officer. We'll be filing charges."

He handed me a business card. I was shaking so hard that I could barely read it.

"A women's shelter?" I asked.

"Call them. They'll help you get a protection from abuse order."

I noticed RJ's coat and shoes were still by the door.

"Won't he need those?" I asked, pointing to them.

The officer looked up, shook his head, and kept writing.

"Where are you taking him?"

"He'll spend the rest of the weekend in jail," he said. "Don't worry. He won't see a judge until at least Monday."

When the police left, I went back to the bedroom, where the girls were playing with Barbies with Dad. I put on a big smile and clapped my hands. "Who wants to go stay at Grandma and Grandpa's?"

They burst into excited laughter.

"Okay! Go with Grandpa and he'll help you get your coats on!"

I knew RJ wouldn't be back that night and we could stay in the house, but my fear was like the reverberating sound of a gong that lingers long after it's been struck. I frantically threw the kids' clothes, toothbrushes, blankies, diapers, and a few toys into a pillowcase and rolled up a few of my immediate necessities in a blanket.

Dad put the girls in my car and buckled their car seats while I put our things in his car.

"It'll be alright, Lynnie," he said, opening my car door.

I just nodded. I was too shocked to cry.

Other than my parents, the only person I told about RJ's violent behavior was the woman who answered the phone at the women's shelter. As I told her what happened, I felt outside my body, like a stranger reciting someone else's story. It sounded so unreal that I started to doubt it. Still, I agreed to meet her at the courthouse on Monday, where she helped me file a protection from abuse order. RJ called that night after being served. His voice was warm and assuring. We didn't need a PFA, he said. He would never hurt me again. He loved me. He needed the girls and me. He promised to stop drinking.

I thought about what he'd said and how he'd said it. Maybe it *was* possible that I'd overreacted, like RJ said I always did. I let him move home, but I didn't feel safe, and I didn't know who to talk to. I was too embarrassed to call the women's shelter again. I mean, all that work they did, and for what?

I considered talking to our pastor, and then I remembered I tried that once. A few days before RJ and I were married, I told him that RJ scared me sometimes. The pastor assured me that RJ would grow out of his "moods" and that I simply had cold feet. Happened to everyone, he said.

Shortly after he moved back home, RJ was working a night

shift. I was channel surfing and landed on a Billy Graham crusade. As a kid, I watched them with my parents. I didn't always understand what he was talking (and sometimes yelling) about from his make-shift, midfield pulpit, but it was clear he knew God better than me, and the energy of the crowd was oddly inspiring.

I wondered if maybe God knew what I should do about RJ. Watching thousands of people stream onto the field to receive Jesus Christ as their savior, I decided to call the prayer hotline scrolling across the screen. A woman answered, and when I told her about RJ and why I was thinking of leaving him, she said the Bible states that, unless he was sexually unfaithful, I had no reason to leave. If I modeled kindness and forgiveness and prayed for him, she assured me God would make everything okay.

As if reading my thoughts, Dr. Angry asks, "Have you considered praying about it? Ask God to help you understand your anger?"

I don't mean to laugh. "If you really want to talk about my anger, we should talk about God, not Bruce or RJ!"

He says that God would never hurt me because God loves me, and God has a plan for what is best for me.

"Forgive my language, but God's 'plan' for me so far has been awfully shitty."

Nonplussed, Dr. Angry looks at me with the same pitiful look I saw on countless faces after Bruce died. "I'm sorry you feel that way."

⊙   ⊙   ⊙

I'd considered quitting therapy, but to get Xanax, I had to keep seeing Dr. Angry. But this week, I stumbled onto a Xanax loophole during a routine gynecology appointment. (Maybe prayer works after all.) I told my doctor how anxious I've been feeling, leaving out the part about the hospital and Dr. Angry. She diagnosed me with severe PMS and wrote me a script for Xanax.

Instead of therapy, I am focusing on the one thing I know I can control: my weight.

I've joined Weight Watchers, although I skip the meetings. I pay the fee, weigh in, and leave. I only eat raw and boiled vegetables, fruit, skim milk, and plain baked white fish. I've quit drinking, and I ride a stationary bike I bought at a garage sale for ten dollars.

It's been four weeks, and I've lost ten pounds. One hundred more to go.

"You'll leave me once you've lost weight," RJ says often.

I assure him I won't.

CHAPTER 19

Driving home from the grocery store, I hear The Pretenders' "Back on the Chain Gang," and a seconds-only memory crystalizes: Bruce and I are standing in the checkout line at the grocery store and "Back on the Chain Gang" is on the overhead speakers. He's singing the "ho-ah" part under his breath as he curls his hand and releases it to the beat.

Music was his life breath.

The evening after we got home from the hospital, Carlene was fussy. I'd fed and changed her, and I must have looked as exhausted as I felt.

"Go to bed. I've got this." Bruce lifted her from my arms and sat in the rocking chair.

Lying in bed, I heard, above Carlene's fuss, the soft creak of the chair keeping time with the song he sang: "You are my sunshine, my only sunshine. You make me happy when skies are gray. You'll never know, dear, how much I love you. Please don't take my sunshine away."

After the second time through, Carlene was asleep. After the third, so was I.

Those really were the happiest days of my life.

I wipe my eyes on my sleeve, hoping the kids won't notice, but of course, Carlene does. Just like her father, she sees things most people overlook and studies me like it's her sixth sense.

"What's wrong, Mama?" she asks from behind the passenger's seat.

Cassie, not yet three, is talking to a book in her lap. "I read, Mama!" she says, peering around my seat.

If Carlene talks, Cassie has to talk, too, whether it makes sense to the conversation or not.

"Good girl, Cass!" I say, smiling at her in the rearview mirror. I reach back and give Carlene's foot a tug. "Nothing's wrong, honey," although I'm still bothered by the dream I had last night that left me so anxious and sad that I'm afraid to go to sleep tonight.

In the dream, I'd found out that Bruce survived the train wreck and was living in a nursing home. My sister-in-law Janice told me he was blind and learning to speak again. I could feel in my sleep how excited I was to see him again. I asked Janice if he remembered me, and she said yes, that he'd asked about me and was wondering where I was.

When I got to the nursing home, I saw him sitting in a wheelchair. He was wearing his red flannel shirt, and his hair was a mess. I tried to move forward, but some invisible force held me back. He couldn't hear me yelling his name, and I thought, *He thinks I've abandoned him!* I felt such intense anguish that when I woke up, my pillow was soaked with tears.

CHAPTER 20

I met a friend at a local bar tonight. It was a welcome change from the evenings spent not talking to RJ. A man across the room bought me a drink.

"He's cute. Go talk to him!" Sara said.

I laughed. "No!"

"Why?"

"Um, because I'm married?"

She sighed. "Are you really?"

It was a valid question. When was the last time RJ and I had fun? We go out for dinner and a movie on Valentine's Day, but more times than not, we greet each other with suspicion and step cautiously around the issue that has plagued our relationship since the beginning: mistrust. When I ask him what he's thinking or where he's been when he comes home late, he says it's none of my business, and every time he says it, I think, *Bruce would never say that to me.*

I went through my closet the other day, sorting through clothes that no longer fit, and, in a heap in the corner, I found Bruce's ratty brown bathrobe. Years ago, the seam around one of the arms had come loose, and I tossed it there thinking that I'd sew it back together one day. I picked it up and put it on. Its weight on my shoulders felt like a hug. I rummaged through the junk drawer and found a needle and thread and repaired the seam with large, crude stitches. Now I wear it after I take a shower.

RJ hasn't mentioned the robe, although before we went to bed last night, during an argument about God knows what, he yelled, "I'm not him!" He didn't say his name, but I knew who he meant.

"Well, 'he's'"—I paused for finger quotes—"none of your business!"

When I went to sleep, I had a Bruce dream. As usual, I found out he was alive, but this time, he was working with his brother John on the family farm. I called him, and he sounded sad. I asked him what happened.

"What do you think happened?" he said sarcastically, which in real life would have been completely out of character. "I got my head smashed in!"

"They didn't tell me what happened!" I cried. "I didn't know what you looked like!"

I convinced him to meet with me, and although he had a gauze bandage wrapped around the top of his head, his eyes were the same warm brown, the color of hot chocolate.

I reached out to touch him, but he pulled away. He said he felt no love, no emotions at all, because that part of his brain was damaged. I said that I was willing to live with that, but he said no, that he was angry and wished he had died rather than be the way he was. I thanked him for Carlene and then suddenly, she walked in the room wearing last year's Christmas dress. Usually, Carlene doesn't show up in my Bruce dreams, and if she does, the two of them don't or can't interact. In this dream, she looked at him and, not knowing who he was, said, "I'm Carly" and disappeared.

I asked him if we could be friends, and he softened a little.

"I just want you to be happy," he said.

I woke up feeling like I'd run a mile and took a few deep breaths to calm my heart rate. I looked over at RJ, who was sleeping, facing the other direction.

Between being haunted by a dead man and living with an erratic one, it's no wonder I'm anxious.

⊙ ⊙ ⊙

Sitting alone on the east beach of Medicine Lake, I watch the sunset through a hazy pink sky. Muffled conversations and laughter float across the bay. Two boats bob a few hundred feet from shore as hopeful fishermen cast their lines one last time.

I wish Bruce was here.

The thought feels rough, selfish, and unfair to RJ, but it's more honest than I've been with myself in a long time. Bruce can't be here, and I don't want RJ here, and no amount of praying will change that.

RJ said I'd leave him when I lost weight, but that's not why I'm considering it. The potential for violence lives on in our home, although these days, RJ is more like a jockey who shows the horse the whip and doesn't use it. I remain cautious, but I'm not as afraid of him as I was. I'm more afraid of what my life will be like if I stay in our marriage.

I don't think my actions will be met with resistance, either by RJ or my mother. I'm pretty sure RJ doesn't like being around me any more than I like being around him, and my mom has witnessed RJ's anger enough times that her larger concern is the safety of my kids and me.

"You're always welcome here," she says each time the kids and I seek refuge.

I study my legs stretched out in the sand. Bird legs, someone called them once, that haven't changed much in one hundred pounds. The rest of me has, especially my attitude. I have aspirations again. I want to do something with my life. Cassie is almost four, Carlene is in kindergarten, and I want them to witness their mother be brave and work for something she wants.

I stand up, brush the sand off my shorts, and shuffle back to the car. Tomorrow is Sunday. I will look through the want ads. I will find a job. And maybe, after that, I'll look into college again.

Part Three

Unintentional Flooding

Wikipedia states, "Flooding . . . is a form of behavior therapy and desensitization—or exposure therapy—based on the principles of respondent conditioning. As a psychotherapeutic technique, it is used to treat phobia and anxiety disorders including post-traumatic stress disorder. It works by exposing the patient to their painful memories, with the goal of reintegrating their repressed emotions with their current awareness. . . . The experience can often be traumatic for a person, but may be necessary if the phobia is causing them significant life disturbances."

CHAPTER 21

1999

Dan, Craig, Steve, another Steve, Patrick, Alex, Mike, John, Tim, Ken, Scott, Paul, a Kevin Costner look-alike, and a UNIX software salesman from Chicago who forgot to tell me he was married with three kids. According to my journal, I dated them all in a one-year, post-RJ frenzy. I remember three of them well, five vaguely, and nine not at all, including the pseudo-Kevin Costner, which is a shame.

I'm not that person anymore. I'm thirty-six and married to my fourth and final husband. He's not Bruce, but that's okay. I stopped looking for him years ago.

Shortly after our divorce was final, RJ married a woman he knew from college and joined the Navy. As their adopted father, he has the right to visit Carlene and Cassie regularly, but it's been ten years since he's seen them. He prefers to drop by my email once in a while to remind me what a terrible mother I am.

Despite what he thinks, the girls are thriving in our small town in western Pennsylvania. We got here thanks to husband number three, Christopher, whom I met in college. After the year of frantic dating, I applied to Augsburg College's weekend program for working adults. Christopher taught the literature class I took during the winter trimester. When it ended in March, he asked me on a date, and we were married eight weeks later. Christopher accepted a teaching position at Clarion University, and we've been here ever since.

Christopher and I were only married for two years. The person I loved was the teacher-performer in front of the classroom. In real life, Christopher is quiet and reclusive, and we have little in common.

Husband number four is Larry. He teaches biochemistry and has two young sons who live with their mother in upstate New York and visit us several times a year. We were married last October and live in a Craftsman-style house with my girls, three dogs, and two cats in a quiet neighborhood.

I am the lifestyles editor, a.k.a. the Good News Lady, for our local paper. I write features about interesting people and take photos of prom queens, county fair blue-ribbon winners, and one-year-olds for the First Birthdays section. I also write a monthly column for the editorial page.

Cassie is in ninth grade, and Carlene is a junior. One of Carlene's graduation requirements is to create a project in which she demonstrates the accumulative knowledge she's gained throughout high school. Some kids raise money for charity, and others perform community service or write a play or song. Carlene wants to write a biography about Bruce.

She looks just like him—same chocolate-brown eyes and hair color, same nose and chin—but she wants to know what he was like before he met me and how, other than physically, they are similar.

Bruce has never been a ghost in our home, but because we were together less than two years, I struggle to answer many of Carlene's questions. She still visits his parents at least once a year, and they talk on the phone several times each month, but Walt and Eileen don't talk about Bruce very often. Bruce's siblings never showed an interest in Carlene, and except for Lisa and Curt, I've lost contact with his friends, so she doesn't know much about her father beyond the scant information his parents and I have shared.

I mention Bruce sometimes in my column when I write within the larger context of grief. Not that I'm a grief guru, but having gone through it and come out the other side, I can write about it with some authority. Mostly, though, I don't think about Bruce as much as I used to, at least not consciously. He still shows up in my dreams once in a while. Several years ago, I caught pieces of a radio interview with a psychic who said that when we dream of the dead, it's their way of communicating with us. I wanted to believe her, but it made no sense that Bruce would invite me into a nightmare, which most of my Bruce dreams are. More likely, as a psychology teacher explained, I have Bruce dreams because I didn't see him dead. My brain is like a needle stuck in the groove of a vinyl record. Because I can't change the fact that I never saw him dead, my brain will forever skip.

It's only October, but Carlene wants to start her project so she can complete it before her senior year, when her schedule will be packed with AP classes, college applications, and lasts—last band concert, last homecoming, last prom, last school play. I help her write letters to the editors of newspapers that serve the Jasper area, asking people who knew Bruce to share their memories with her. I warn her that it's been nearly seventeen years since the accident and that it was possible, even probable, that few people who knew him would read the letter or remember him very well.

Still, I'm hopeful she'll get a few responses. It will be fun getting to know him a little better.

⊙ ⊙ ⊙

Less than a week after her letter ran in the papers, Carlene receives a manilla envelope from Bruce's second-grade teacher, Mrs. Anderson. Inside, among other things, is a copy of his second-grade photo and a get-well letter he sent to her when she was recovering from an illness. It's dated March 7, 1967, a week shy of his eighth birthday.

"'Dear Mrs. Anderson,'" Carlene reads out loud, "'I hope you are feeling well. At home, our cousins came, and my nephew messed up the house, so then we had to clean it up again. After supper, we watched the Monkees. Your friend, Bruce.'"

Walt's birthday is March 6, and the family gets together for dinner each year on the Sunday before.

"That must be why everyone was at the house," I tell Carlene, rereading the note. "The last birthday dinner I was at was five days before you were born. Your dad and I were relegated to the kids' table in the kitchen, as always."

Carlene laughs because she never sits at the kids' table. No matter her age, Grandma Eileen always insists she sits next to her at every Bouwman gathering.

"You know your cousin Wendell's a month older than me, right?" I continue. "That's probably the messy nephew he meant. Anyway, after dinner that day, when the adults were in the living room and the rest of us were in the family room, your dad walked over to Walt's recliner and sat down, and then he slapped his lap for me to take a seat. I eased my butt down and threw my legs over the armrest. He wrapped his arms around me and . . . well . . . you, too, I guess."

Another memory steps in line with the other. Walt had walked through the family room, perhaps on his way to the bathroom, and he'd asked me how I was feeling and wished me good luck.

"Your dad and I looked at each other like, 'What just happened?' Grandpa could be tough."

The Grandpa Walt that Carlene knows is a marshmallow. Maybe in a few years, I'll tell her our backstory, how we struggled to live in each other's presence when I joined the family, but for now, he'll remain the lovestruck old man who'd do anything for his granddaughter.

Carlene unfolds a playbill Mrs. Anderson included from *A Feudin' Over Yonder*, the play in which Bruce had been cast as the lead in February 1983. He died two weeks before its run, and the play was postponed for several weeks so his alternate could learn the part. On the back page is a tribute to Bruce: "We who are involved with this production feel sorrow at the loss of our friend and co-worker. We would like to present this play in loving memory of a young man who shared himself and touched our lives."

Carlene starts reading the letter from Mrs. Anderson. "Listen to this. 'Bruce made a banana cake and a thermos of coffee and brought them to play practice on his birthday.'"

"Oh, yeah! I forgot. Someone told me about it a few weeks after the funeral." Bruce had turned twenty-four a few days after Carlene was born. It snowed heavily that day, so he couldn't get to the hospital, and he didn't mention the cake when he called me that night. "I remember buying that cake mix at the grocery store. How weird is that?"

I can see our kitchen clearly as I imagine Bruce making a cake. He takes the eggs out of the fridge, grabs the oil from above the stove, opens the drawer where I keep the measuring cups, searches for the cake pan, and probably at some point wonders where I put the pot holders, then uses a towel instead to get the cake out of the oven. I wonder if he made the coffee strong like he preferred or with one less scoop in deference to the others.

"Yeah, your dad was a nice guy." I wipe away a tear. "Did I ever tell you about Valentine's Day the year you were born?"

Carlene shakes her head no.

Bruce had said he was going to town after lunch. God knows it was probably snowing and a hundred degrees below zero outside, so I didn't ask to go along. After he left, I went to the living room to watch *All My Children*. I heard him come back in the house through the mudroom and go down to the basement. I didn't say anything because it felt personal, like if he wanted me to know he was there, he'd have said something. I heard him rummage around for a minute and leave again. When he came home, he handed me the bud vase from the basement with two roses inside.

"He gave me a card, too. I have it somewhere. I kept all his letters."

"Can I read them?"

"I'll have to read them again first. I'm pretty sure there are things in a few of them you don't want to know about."

"Ew, Mom!" Carlene wrinkles her nose. "Gross!"

"Hey, we had a lot of fun together! How do you think you got here?"

She raises her hand. "I don't want to hear it again!"

What she doesn't want to hear again is how our attempts to get pregnant in the four months after the miscarriage had failed. When Bruce threw out his back and was taking a muscle relaxant, I didn't want to wait another month, so I poured him a glass of blackberry brandy and brought it to him as he lay prone in bed.

"Here, drink this," I'd said.

He set down the book he was reading.

"Are you trying to seduce me, Mrs. Bouwman?"

I kissed him as I unzipped my jeans.

"Maybe . . ."

⊙ ⊙ ⊙

As if his friends were waiting for an invitation to tell her about her father, Carlene receives another twenty emails and letters within a week.

Some describe him as conscientious and encouraging. One person noted, "Bruce had a sense of significance. He acted as if each decision involved more than just himself. It was so unusual as a teenager."

Someone else sent a piece of sheet music she'd kept from a wedding at which she'd accompanied Bruce on the organ. "I remember having a lot of fun practicing this song with Bruce. It's difficult for me to give up this piece of music since it brings me back to that time in my life, but after seeing your article in the paper, I feel it may mean a lot to you. Not only was Bruce very talented, but he was a fun, upbeat person to be around."

Others write about specific memories from grade school, playing on the varsity football team, singing with Bruce in choir and choral competitions. His closest friends remember hanging out, drinking beer, listening to music, and watching *Saturday Night Live*. One friend tells a story about how, when Bruce was eighteen, he snuck his underage friends into a drive-in showing the X-rated movie *Pom-Pom Girls*.

"'He was worried that if we got caught, they would kick us out, and he wouldn't get to see the movie!'" I read out loud. "See? I told you! Your dad was just bad enough to not be perfect."

The woman who inspired Carlene's name sends an email, too: "As you have noticed, we share a very unique first name. I was living in Montana at the time you were born and remember it very well. My mom called me right away because of your name."

The first formal occasion Bruce and I attended together was his friend Carlene's wedding. I sat in the back of the church, and he sat in the front because he was the vocalist. Driving to the church, he told me that he would look at me when he sang, and when he did, I felt like I was the only one there. It didn't matter that the song was a hymn. To me, it was a love song.

When Bruce and I talked about what to name the baby, I wanted to name a girl Miranda, and Bruce wanted the name

Carlene. I thought that was sweet, but I really liked the name Miranda. After Bruce cut his unnamed daughter's umbilical cord, a nurse wrapped her up and handed her to him. While a doctor stitched my parts back together and asked if he could plant my placenta in his rose garden, Bruce looked at me with tears running down his face and said, "Can we name her Carlene?"

I didn't say no to either of them.

CHAPTER 22

One email sums up best what many others thought when they learned Bruce died:

> It's amazing how people will remember so much of a single moment in their life. It's like a picture was taken when I heard your dad died. God, it was so tragic. I thought about you and your mom for days and how devastating it must be to your mom.
>
> This is still hard to write about. We all missed out on a lot since Bruce was killed. What would have been different if he were still here? Watch It's a Wonderful Life. I wonder how much better things would be in Jasper if he was still here?

The email is from Sam.

Just seeing his name, I feel a toxic mix of joy and regret.

After our one drunken night together two months after Bruce died, I didn't see Sam again for six years. I'd only gone to Jasper twice after Cassie was born, both times for a funeral.

Buffered by time, Jasper was no longer an emotional behemoth, so just before I started college, I took a weekend trip to visit my grandmothers and Lisa and Curt.

Driving into town, I passed Sam's auto repair shop. Creeping along the street, I felt like a nervous teenager. *Should I stop? Nah, he won't remember me. Wait, no, go, you look cute!*

I jerked the car into a parking space on the street, checked my teeth in the rearview, and walked into the bay where Sam was lying on a creeper under a car.

"Sam?"

"Just a . . . minute," he grunted. "I just have to . . . there."

He rolled out from under the car and saw my bare legs. He slowly took in the rest of me until his eyes landed on my face. It was exactly the reaction I'd hoped for.

"Hey . . ."

"Hi," I said, my insides on fire. "It's good to see you."

He got up and approached me with his arms outstretched. "Good to see you, too!"

I hesitated, and he looked down at the grease on his coveralls. He stepped away and offered a quick wave instead.

"Let's . . ."—he looked around for a towel to wipe his hands— "let's go talk in the office."

I sat down on a chair in front of his desk. He sat down in his chair, smiled again, and shook his head. "Oh, my God, how long has it been?"

"Um . . . I don't know. Six years, I think?"

"Well, you look great! How've you been?"

"I'm good! How've you been?"

"Good, good. I saw your aunt Mavis the other day. She's doing good."

"Yeah, she is. It's been a while since I've seen her. I thought it was time."

"Katinka's still in the apartments, right?"

"Yeah, so is Signe. I'll see them all tomorrow."

"You know, ah . . ." He cleared his throat. "I'm having a few people over tonight. I think Curt and Lisa are coming. Would you like to come?"

I immediately started planning what to wear.

"I'm staying with them this weekend," I said. "I'd love to see your house! It's finished, right?"

When Bruce was alive, Sam bought a few acres outside of Jasper. After the basement was dug, he made it into a temporary living space until he could afford to complete the rest. That's the place I remembered, the place I'd been twice: once with Bruce and once by myself.

"Yeah, I finished it a few years ago," he said and went on to describe it. Listening to him talk made me buzzy and crush-happy for the first time in years.

What felt like a few minutes was actually an hour, and when I looked at my watch, I realized I needed to go. As I stood to leave, I said, "I'll see you tonight!"

"Great!" he replied with a wink. "It'll be fun!"

⊙ ⊙ ⊙

Sam met us at the door, and I gazed around the open, spacious layout. "Wow! It's . . . stunning!"

His house reflected how we'd all matured from the days of basement parties. New furniture versus parents' hand-me-downs, French doors versus egress windows, a gas range versus a hot plate, bottles versus keg.

I stepped down into the sunken living room and sat on the couch. Sam handed everyone a beer and sat down opposite of me. There were four other people in the room, but we paid close attention to each other. After a few hours, Lisa and Curt needed to go home to their children, and Sam leaned in and whispered, "Stay a while longer. I'll take you back to their house later."

Unlike the last time we were together, when grief was raw and hung like a veil between us, it was just Sam and me: our bodies, our breath, and our laughter. We watched the sun come up over the cornfield that bordered his backyard, and I felt none of the guilt I felt the first time, no need to confess.

"Come back tonight?" he whispered, his arms wrapped around my lower back.

"Yes."

Over the next few months, I snuck into Jasper a few more times to see Sam, and each time, I parked my car in his garage, since it was inevitable that someone would see a strange car in his driveway and either stop to see who was there or later pepper him with questions that he didn't want to answer. We wanted this, whatever "this" was, to remain our secret. The problem, at least for me, wasn't keeping it a secret. The problem was keeping my feelings casual.

The last time I saw Sam, I'd already met Christopher. Sam met me for dinner in Mankato, a few hours' drive for each of us, and we immediately fell into our familiar rhythm. After dinner, we walked around town. His smile sparked the same feelings that brought me to his bed all those times before.

"Do you want to come up?" I asked when we got to my hotel.

His mouth was warm and comforting, his touch electric, but when we fell into bed, I couldn't do anything more. A warning light went off in my head, alerting me that I'd seamlessly crossed the one emotional line that I never wanted to cross again. Love like that hurt so much when I lost Bruce that there was no way I was putting my hand over that flame again.

"I can't" was the only explanation I offered before curling up in a ball under the sheet. Sam didn't say anything and soon, I fell asleep. When I woke up, he was gone. I called him, but I still couldn't tell him how I felt. After a long silence, he said he couldn't do "this" anymore, that he needed to move on. It was the last time we talked.

Seeing his name on the email, I feel as hollow as I did in that moment in the hotel. I want to tell him that I am sorry and explain how scared I was back then, but what good could that do? Like Bruce's death, what happened had happened; what was done was done. Nothing I say or do can change anything.

"Thank you for your email. It was good to hear from you," I write back. "I hope you're doing well. Lynn."

CHAPTER 23

Other than her grandmother, the only person from Bruce's family to contact Carlene is his nephew Jason, John's son, who was fifteen when Bruce died.

Dear Carlene, I read your letter in the *Jasper Journal* this afternoon.

Bruce was more like a big brother to me than an uncle. We were nine years apart and it made for some very enjoyable and somewhat competitive games (basketball, football, softball, etc.) during the summers. I know now that he would hold back and let me occasionally win, but when I was able to beat my uncle at anything athletic, it was a BIG thing for me.

I remember the last thing I did with Bruce. We were at a church outing in Pipestone at the local rec center. We were playing basketball with some other guys. I remember getting mad at him for some reason during the game (I can't remember why I was mad at him) and that was the last time I saw him. It still bothers me that the last time I saw him was when I was disagreeing with him.

I don't know how much you want to read about my experiences with Bruce, but he was a tremendously positive influence on me. He was there when I needed fatherly advice but was too embarrassed to ask my dad. He was there to explain things that

I didn't fully understand. He was what I hoped I could grow up

to become. I thought so much of Uncle Bruce that I wanted to
name my son after him. It was a losing battle, though.

I remember the day he died and the days following. I was in
school and another student came up to me and asked, 'Why are
you still in school? Didn't you hear . . .' The last sentence was
never finished. I found out minutes later what she was trying
to tell me when the principal asked to see me in his office. I
remember that day like it was last week. A few days later in the
funeral home, I just couldn't hold my emotions in any longer.

I wandered around Jasper alone for hours, crying more than I
thought humanly possible. (I am tearing up as I write this.) I had
lost more than an uncle. I had lost someone who I considered
one of my best friends.

I am grateful for Jason's email, yet it picks at a festering wound.
Bruce was the emotional black sheep of the family. Unlike many in
his family, he wasn't afraid to express his love and care for others.
It would seem Jason inherited the same quality. When Bruce's
brothers and sister didn't initiate a relationship with Carlene
after he died, I first thought it was because Bruce and I weren't
together long enough for family loyalty or affinity to solidify. Then
I thought how, if my brother Matthew died, I would do everything
I could to maintain my relationship with his children, and how, if
it had been one of his siblings who died, Bruce would have stayed
close to his nieces and nephews, too.

Perhaps their inaction is spurred by grief. Perhaps it's stoic
Midwest suspicion of emotions—you don't go around bothering
other people with your feelings. Still, as Carlene's mother, it's
hard to understand why most of Bruce's family choose not to
know her.

⊙ ⊙ ⊙

A former neighbor writes how she and Bruce rode the bus to school together and that sometimes they'd walk down to the creek near their farms and throw rocks in the water. They talked about school and baseball and, something I was not aware of, her brother, who died in a car-train wreck in 1971.

"Wayne's death seemed to bother Bruce, and we talked about it many times; I in grief, he in curious compassion. Ironically, his life would end at the same spot."

Questions resurface that I haven't asked in years—fruitless questions that do nothing more than upset me—and I fantasize about the "why" and "what ifs." Why didn't Bruce hear the train? What if he'd seen the train and stopped? Where would we be today?

With every email and letter, I bounce between solidarity with the writer and feeling cheated. Learning of the breadth of others' grief is oddly comforting, knowing I wasn't the only one who missed Bruce and that his death changed each of us. At the same time, I envy their memories and am reminded of how little time we had together.

Years ago, when Dr. Angry said it was normal to be angry at Bruce for dying, especially for how he died, I hated him for suggesting it. I loved Bruce and felt sad for him and sad for me. Anger, I insisted, was the antithesis of love, which was the antithesis of grief. Dr. Angry disagreed, yet nothing he said changed my mind. But maybe he was right. Seventeen years later and I'm asking the same questions, paired with the same angry feelings. I wonder if I should talk to someone after Carlene's project is complete, but mostly, I hope that all the feelings that have emerged will go back to where I put them years ago.

CHAPTER 24

Carlene only knows her father through the voices of others, which makes the latest contributions to Carlene's project so significant.

Both offer her Bruce's voice.

The first is through a letter. It begins: "My name is Mary . . ."

The last time I saw Mary, I was sitting in the middle of the front seat of the black Chrysler parked behind the hearse. I'd looked away when they brought out Bruce's casket, and I saw Mary walking across the street. I remember thinking, *This could have been you. I wish it was you.*

"I first got to know your father at the beginning of his senior year in high school."

The year he played Curly in *Oklahoma!*

"We met at a party. It seems almost silly to say that we 'met' there because in such a small town, everyone knew everyone else, but it was the first time that he really talked to me. I was just a sophomore at the time, so of course, I was thrilled that he even spoke to me! And I was in love right away."

I fell in love with him that year, too, only he had no idea who I was.

"He picked me up in his freshly washed brown Monte Carlo. He loved that car!"

Bruce talked about that car like it was a god. I only knew him after he bought the Citation.

"We dated steadily for the rest of that school year and through the next summer. When he went to college in the fall, we began to drift apart."

Bruce told me about the girls he'd dated, including Mary, and

I was jealous of them all. But on the day of his funeral, watching Mary walk away from the church, I wasn't jealous. I was angry. I thought, *If Mary and Bruce had stayed together, Mary's husband would be the one being rolled into the belly of a hearse, and I'd be anywhere but here!* But as soon as the thought was out of my head, I felt awful. Mary lost a friend, and that was sufficient grief. I couldn't wish what I was going through on her. And if she had been in the front seat, I wouldn't have had twenty-one months with Bruce, and I wouldn't have Carlene.

Still, Mary's email tugs at my heart, like I'm still that insecure nineteen-year old.

"We corresponded throughout that year, and I still have several of the letters. If you'd like, I could send you some of them that might give you a feel for what he was thinking at the time."

Carlene is reading Mary's email over my shoulder. "I'd really like to read those letters. Would you mind?"

My heart sinks to my toes. *What if he wrote the same things to her that he wrote to me? What if I wasn't that special after all? What if I was just another girl?*

"No, honey, I don't mind," I say. "Let Mary know you'd like to read them."

A few weeks later, Mary sends Carlene several letters, and even though I only read one (it's all my jealous heart could stand), I assure Carlene that the voice in the letter is indeed her father's.

The second voice comes in a large envelope from Bob Jones, Jasper High School's former choir director. Inside are two cassette tapes. Of all the weddings and concerts in which Bruce performed solo, no one so far had produced a recording. I even called someone who used to work at the high school to ask if any of the plays or musicals had been recorded, but he said no, the tapes and film had been reused.

I haven't heard Bruce's voice since the day he died, and I wonder if I'll recognize it. My hands shake as I put the first tape in the player. I look at Carlene. Her face is alive with excitement and anticipation. I take a deep breath and press play.

"You're not supposed to have favorites when you're teaching . . ."

I hit pause and exhale.

"Okay, that's Bob's voice, obviously," I say nervously and press play again.

". . . but Bruce was one of my all-time favorites, and as far as vocal music is concerned, probably my best performer. As far as his personality, Carlene, your dad . . . he was always with a ready smile, very polite, very positive, calm, and really quite unflappable. I wish I had some of those characteristics.

"Along with the program from Lil Abner, I'm sending a very poor tape of a rehearsal we had for *Oklahoma!* Keep in mind that this was a number of years ago, and it was a little handheld tape recorder and on a stage with a lot of activity. Much of the voice is lost, but at least you have an inkling of what Bruce sounded like. Hope you enjoy it."

How ironic that "Curly" had no idea I existed, and now, twenty-two years since the play, I am his widow and the mother of his child and standing in a living room in western Pennsylvania holding a tape of him singing "The Surrey with the Fringe on Top."

I am excited, but at the same time, I feel like I'm holding a pull cord to a net filled with pieces of grief-shaped confetti that, when opened, will bury me in pain. I consider asking Carlene to listen to the recording by herself, and then I think about how I've witnessed so many of her firsts: first words, first step, first day of school, first date. I don't want to miss the first time she hears her father's voice.

I put the tape in the deck and press play. The rotating heads squeak and hesitate, and seconds later, just as Bob described, we hear the raucous sound of teenagers and a pit band rehearsing. Then, like fine-tuning a radio station, I pull Bruce's voice out of the chaos, and it spreads out like a warm blanket. His tenor voice is robust and animated and, thankfully, familiar.

Carlene has seen images, read stories, and handled tangible pieces of physical evidence that her father had once been alive, but he's never been a part of the family. She is a Bouwman. Her grandparents, uncles, aunts, and cousins are Bouwmans. But Bruce, in his absence, isn't. He is a face in a photo that looks a lot like her, but he isn't a member of the family who shares her name. Finally, by hearing his voice, he becomes real.

"I've never had the whole package, Mom," Carlene whispers.

I had a Bruce dream a few months ago, a rare happy one. Bruce and I were sitting in the Jasper High School auditorium watching a play, and even though I knew he was going to die, when he smiled at me, the happy I felt was real, as real as the happy I feel now, listening to him singing in our living room.

CHAPTER 25

I felt like Nancy Drew when I went to the newspaper office a few months after Bruce died and requested the photos and negatives of the accident. Because I couldn't unsee what they'd printed in the paper, I decided I would do everything I could to make sure no one else would see them again, either. I explained that I needed them for a lawsuit and would return them as soon as possible, even though there was never going to be a lawsuit and I had no intention of returning them.

Even now, it feels like a small victory.

Carlene has always known I have the photographs, and if I had my way, she'd never see them, but when she called the Pipestone County Historical Society last week and requested photocopies of the newspaper accounts of the accident, as well as every reference to her father and me from 1982 and 1983, I thought it was best if she looked at the actual photos with me before she saw them in the context of a newspaper story.

While she's in school, I dig out the photos from the bottom of a storage bin in which I keep mostly happy memories. I take the photos out of the envelope they've been in for seventeen years. They are as crisp and shiny as the day I took them from the newspaper office.

The day Bruce died was sunny, but in black and white, the photos reflect the stark, violent aftermath of a train-tractor crash, and looking through them, I feel the emotion they captured. They are the closest thing I have to actually being there, like they are perverse "wish you were here!" postcards. I examine the photos carefully, top to bottom, and in one, I recognize a man standing a few feet from Bruce's body.

My mind races. *I know him . . . he's married to—what's her name? She worked at our grocery store. I used to babysit their kids. Dad, Matthew, and I had dinner at their house when Mom was in the hospital having Emily.*

When I was twelve, he watched our black lab, Barney, when we went on vacation. The vacation when Barney died. Barney was terrified of thunder, and there was a thunderstorm one night, and he died alone in his doghouse. He called the resort to tell Dad, and he said the vet believed Barney had a heart condition. When we got home, I went to Barney's doghouse and opened the top and saw the imprint of his body in the straw. How scared he must have been! If only I'd been there! I'd have gone outside and brought him to the garage, or maybe Mom and Dad would have let me bring him into the laundry room, and we would have rode out the storm together.

That man saw my dog dead.

That man saw my husband dead.

And that man never talked to me about either one.

I place the photos back in the envelope. When Carlene and I look through them later, I won't mention the man in the photo or Barney. She will feel sad enough without knowing those parts.

⊙ ⊙ ⊙

I am surprised by the number of newspaper photocopies that arrive from the historical society. Carlene and I go through them in chronological order. The first is our engagement announcement. Carlene reads it out loud.

"Oh, man." I laugh. "That was me marking my territory. Hands off, ladies!"

The next one is my church bridal shower announcement. My friends and family had thrown me a shower in Minneapolis, and Bruce's family threw me a shower in Iowa, but Signe insisted on throwing me a traditional church bridal shower, too. While I didn't want one, it meant a lot to Signe.

"So, I did what other Jasper American Lutheran brides-to-be did," I tell Carlene. "I went to Our Own Hardware and picked out a few things, what we call a gift registry now."

I explain how women from church would go to the store and put a few dollars on an item from a bride's list and sign their names on a card, usually Mrs. Husband's name. The money they spent on showers went around and around. One woman's daughter or granddaughter would get engaged, and the other women would put two dollars on a steak knife set. Then when another woman's daughter or granddaughter got married, the others would put two dollars on a hamper.

We page through the next paper, which features a story about *Feudin' Over Yonder* with a photo of Bruce hugging the woman who played his character's wife. Jody was a pastor's wife and not an ex-girlfriend, so I was fine with the hug when I first saw the picture. Well, mostly.

The next paper contains Carlene's birth announcement, and the final one includes the accident and Bruce's obituary. As Carlene reads the accident story out loud, I feel a familiar sting of shock, muted somewhat by the years, but painful, nonetheless. My stomach begins to churn, and my heart begins to race. I don't want Carlene to witness me having a panic attack, so I ask her to take the package to her bedroom.

"We can talk more about this later," I assure her.

"Are you okay, Mama?"

I force a smile. "I'll be fine. This is all just a little harder than I expected."

With Carlene in her room on the first floor, I go to my office on the third floor, collapse in a chair, and cry into a pillow. My emotions are balled up like a knotted necklace, and I don't know how to begin to untangle them all. I reach in my desk drawer and take out a bottle of Xanax. I've taken it more frequently the last few months, and there are only a few left. I swallow one dry and take out another. I know I'll be groggy tomorrow, and tomorrow is a deadline day at work, but I swallow it anyway.

Waking the next morning with a Xanax hangover, I lick the fuzz from my mouth and look at the clock. I'll make it to work on time if I skip the shower.

I walk in the newsroom and set my bag on my desk. Before I start, I'll need coffee.

"I'm going to Michelle's Café. Anyone want anything?" I ask the room. "Rodney?"

Rodney, the editor, is the only person who looks up from their keyboard. "Oh, um, no, babe, I'm fine."

"Okay, I'll be right back."

I return with a cup full of enough caffeine to get me through some quick edits and laying out my sections before the noon deadline. I thrive working on a deadline, and after I run the pages upstairs to the composing director, I usually feel satisfied with my work. Today, though, I'm irritated and jittery and it has nothing to do with the coffee. I can't stop thinking about the accident photos in the paper.

I call to Rodney across the aisle. "Would you run a photo of a dead body?"

Rodney knows how Bruce died. He'd found out while he was working on a story about the new fiberboard plant. The owners had wanted to utilize an old railroad bed that ran across a heavily trafficked road, only they had no plans for crossing lights. Rodney was telling everyone in the newsroom about it when he asked, "Any bets on when the first person gets killed by a train?"

We bet on everything in the newsroom: which couples in the engagement section were pregnant, which couples in the wedding announcements would get divorced, which magistrate's office would report the highest blood-alcohol levels that week. Nothing was off limits, including death.

I raised my hand. "Um, Rodney? My husband was killed by a train."

The room fell silent. Rodney's face turned sober.

"What? No, you're . . . ha! You're kidding, right?"

"No, I'm serious. Carlene's dad. He was crossing the tracks in his tractor and was hit by a train."

"Oh, shit," I heard another reporter say under his breath.

"Lynn—" Rodney shook his head. "Oh, Lynn. Damn, I'm really sorry. I feel terrible."

"No, no, it's okay!" I assured him. "It was a long time ago!"

The silence was awkward.

"Really," I said. "I'm okay. Take the bet."

As far as I know, that bet didn't fly.

Rodney leans back in his chair. "Two incidents affect my answer. One, when I first started here, like my second week on the job, I was working alone on a Sunday afternoon. The scanner went off with a report of a shooting. They said the name of the victim, and I knew the name, so I went to the scene. Turns out it wasn't the person I knew. I took a photo of the body lying in a dump with a state trooper and the coroner standing over it. I developed the film and printed out a photo and was a little apprehensive about it. The editor at the time printed it over my objections. I wish I'd never told him I had it. I felt sick for being responsible for the victim's family seeing him lying in the trash and garbage of a rural illegal dumpsite.

"Two, a traffic crash. I only took the photo because I was coming back from town and encountered it. I was the editor then and decided to print it. His mother called me, screaming in her pain and loss. I haven't gone to a car crash since.

"The public has the right to know about a fatal crash. It's

news. It can be a lesson. It can lead to a call for improvements or change. But there is no right to see the deceased in a gory photo that only hurts the living. Everyone has a right to a little dignity, even the dead. So, no, I would never run a photo of a body ever again."

His answer emboldens me. I put on my coat and gather my things. "I have to take care of something."

I go home and call the newspaper in Minnesota. I ask for the editor, and when he answers, I tell him who I am.

"Oh, hello!" he says. "I've been wondering how your daughter's project is coming along. Has her letter been effective?"

This disarms me.

"Yeah, um . . . she's had an overwhelming response, more than we expected."

"Good! I'm glad we could help."

"Yes, but . . ." My voice starts to waiver. "I was looking at the newspaper story of Bruce's accident, and I need to ask, why did you print the photo of his body under that tarp?"

He is quiet for a moment.

"I'm sorry about that," he says. "I truly am. I was the sports editor at the time, and I remember telling the editor that it was a bad idea to print that photo, and he did it anyway. We got a lot of mail about it, all of it angry."

"Yeah, I imagine you did. And that's why . . . that's why . . ."

What I thought would feel good, like a release, doesn't feel right anymore. Unleashing my anger on this man—blaming him for my pain—won't make my heart less heavy. Bruce will still be dead.

"Never mind. Thank you for talking to me."

"Sure, not a problem," he says. "Best of luck to your daughter, and let me know—"

I hang up before he can hear me crying.

CHAPTER 26

Five months after her project started, when we think there is nothing more anyone wants to say, Carlene receives one more email.

Dearest Carlene (and Lynn),

As I sit here at my computer, I have in front of me the bulletin from the funeral service for Bruce. I often think of that week in the life of the Jasper community because it was filled with some of the most profound pain and sorrow I have ever witnessed. Your dad belonged to those people, and his death was deeply felt by all who knew him.

Looking back, I also remember one of the greatest errors we made in those days was not letting your mother at least touch some portion of his body. It was not fair of us (the mortician and me) to not make it possible for this physical ending to happen. How difficult it must have been to have Bruce virtually disappear from her life. My deepest apologies for this mistake.

Sincerely, David Mohn, former pastor
of the American Lutheran Church

Like Bruce's letter, the one in which he used the word "adjust" to describe how a character in a play learned to live with her husband's death, I consider David's word choices. "Difficult" and "mistake" are surface-scratcher words, minor players in the lexicon of emotional descriptors. "Difficult" is your goldfish dying when you're six years old. "Mistake" is taking a wrong turn or dialing a wrong number. Neither word can begin to describe the last seventeen years.

I was raised to trust religious figureheads, and I'd trusted David like I was a lost puppy. When I asked him if I could see Bruce, I believed him when he said it wasn't a good idea. "Remember him as he was alive," he told me. And alive is where Bruce has remained in my brain, which still wonders, *Where did he go?*

David told me after Bruce's funeral that no matter how many years passed, I would be able to recall that time and feel everything all over again. He was right because, after reading his email, I feel exactly like I did then, only now, nearly twice my age later, I have a word for it: neutered. It didn't matter to anyone that I was Bruce's wife: not David, not the funeral director, not even Bruce's brother John. By "not letting" me touch a portion of his body or to see his entire body if I wanted, they usurped my authority. But at nineteen, I didn't know how to speak from authority because I didn't know I had any.

Although I appreciate that at least one of them who kept me from seeing Bruce has acknowledged they were wrong, I doubt an apology will convince my brain that he's dead and make the nightmares stop.

I'm shaking and on the verge of another panic attack. I take two Xanax and decide I will write to David when I'm not so upset, when I can find the right words.

CHAPTER 27

Early one morning, a few weeks after school let out for the summer, Carlene's friend Cheryl calls. Without saying hello to me, she asks if she can talk to Carlene.

I tell her she's sleeping. "Can I have her call you back when she wakes up?"

"It's really important, Lynn," she pleads. "Can you wake her up?"

Important to a seventeen-year-old girl is different than important to a thirty-six-year-old woman, but I figure I'll let Carlene chew out Cheryl for waking her up. I go downstairs to her room, wake her up, and hand her the phone.

A few minutes later, Carlene comes upstairs, pale as a sheet.

"Did you hear sirens this morning?" she asks.

I had, but that was nothing new. They wail nearly every day due to the frequency of accidents on Interstate 80.

She starts to cry. "Cheryl heard Tony was killed."

Tony is Cassie's and Carlene's and everyone's best friend. He was in my kitchen just a few days earlier, eating my food and calling me "Mom," like he always does.

Rumors like this are almost always true, especially in small towns.

"I'll call the paper and see what they know."

I dial the phone. "Hey, it's Lynn. I heard there was an accident this morning. Do you know anything?"

Carlene watches as I nod my head.

"So, it was Tony?" More nodding. "Okay, thanks."

"Mommy, oh, my God!"

I wrap her in my arms as she sobs. "Why? Why?"

"Shhh, shhh, honey," I whisper, stroking her hair and thinking, *How in the hell am I going to tell Cassie?*

Carlene goes limp as her tears subside. "Go get dressed," I tell her. "Your friends will need you, and you'll need them. I'll find out where everyone is gathering."

As Carlene walks down the stairs, I walk into the living room, phone in hand, and sit down on the couch. I have to call my sister Emily. It's 7 a.m. in California. Cassie will be sleeping.

Cassie is our file clerk at the paper, and she'd saved for months to buy a ticket to visit her aunt. She was supposed to be there for two weeks. She's been there two days.

"Em? Em, I know it's early."

"No, no, it's okay. What's wrong?"

I tell her about Tony. "Cass has to come home."

"Of course, of course," she says. "I'll take care of that."

"Okay, thank you." I take a deep breath. "Now—can you wake her up?"

As Emily walks to the guest room, I think about my mother and the day Bruce died and how I never imagined I'd be in a similar situation.

"Lynn, Mavis is on the phone," Mom had said, her hand covering the receiver. "Is Bruce here?"

"He's in the machine shed, I think." I opened the front door and saw the train was still stopped on the tracks. Our dog, Duke, was lying on the stoop.

"Bruce!" I called out. Except for a few birds chirping, everything was quiet. "Bruce?"

I shut the door.

"I'll put on my boots and—" I said, but Mom had returned to her conversation with Mavis.

"Okay, yes. I understand," Mom said and hung up.

"Lynnie—" she said, her eyes filling with tears. "There's been an accident—"

I hear Emily open a door. "Cassie?" she says. "Sweetie? Wake up. Your mom needs to talk to you."

"Mom?" Cassie says in a sleep voice.

"Cassie," I say. "There's been an accident—"

⊙ ⊙ ⊙

Carlene is no longer on the outside of her senior project. She knows too well what everyone expressed in their letters and emails and pieces of Bruce, that when someone you love dies, you feel unimaginable things, and you can never be the same person you were the minute before you found out.

In November, I attend Carlene's project assessment. My heart aches for her as she reads her summary:

> When my father died, the whole town went into mourning. That wasn't hard for me to imagine because, the day Tony died, I fully understood the devastation of losing someone close. Tony was so dear to me. He knew everything about me. Tony was a friend to everyone. His accident shook the whole community, and thinking of him still makes me cry. I get so sad some days and wonder why something so horrible had to happen. In so many ways, Tony was like my father, and if they had the chance to meet here on Earth, they'd be great friends. I know, in Heaven, they're together, which comforts me some. I trust my father, and I know he's taking good care of Tony.

While I don't share Carlene's perception of heaven, I wrote a column about Tony a few weeks after he died, knowing that people were seeking comfort, not a theology lesson:

> The last time I saw Tony alive was two days before he died,

when he stopped by our house to say hi. We sat on the porch, and I don't remember what we talked about, but he was happy, and after his signature hug, his aftershave clung to me for hours. Tony's visits were always a joy. I never imagined that was the last one.

Three nights later, I sat on the porch getting reacquainted with a familiar and unwelcome heartache, and I thought about duality and how our souls can know sadness and joy at the same time, and how sometimes they are the same feeling. It's the only way I can explain the pain of losing Tony at the same time as the joy of knowing him.

The elusive question, Why? hung in the air, and I asked the heavens, Where is God? Heaven replied, 'Weeping beside all of you who grieve.' I forget that sometimes, especially when the pain of grief, present and past, is so crushing. God is not sadistic or self-important. God doesn't pluck people out to serve him, at least not at the expense of his children. The grace of God is in how we comfort and love one another.

In college, I majored in English and minored in religion. Studying feminist and liberation theology, I replaced the gray-haired, old-man-in-the-sky God with a God rooted in social justice, a God that could withstand questions without retaliation. I stopped blaming God for Bruce's death and stopped wondering if Bruce's death was a divine punishment, test of faith, or demonstration of strength. But I also stopped believing that God wept with us when we grieved. Instead, God was the blankie I slept with until I was in sixth grade. It was a rag of a thing, threadbare after eleven years. I came home from school one day, and Mom had thrown it away. She said I didn't need it anymore.

Needing God never got me anywhere. I still had massive panic attacks. I still spent nights sobbing. I still felt untethered and lost, and I still made stupid decisions. In separating from God, I learned that all I needed was me. And Xanax, once in a while.

⊙ ⊙ ⊙

"Death is exhausting," I tell my doctor. She wanted to see me in person before renewing my Xanax prescription. "I'm tired of talking about it, and I'm tired of hearing about it. I'm especially tired of crying over it."

She takes out her prescription pad. "I'm writing you a script for an antidepressant, which should also help with the anxiety. I also want you to see a therapist."

"Can I see what happens with the meds first?"

She hands me the script. "At least give it some thought. I want to see you again in six weeks."

"Paxil?" I ask, reading the paper.

"I think you'll do well with it, although it takes about six weeks to reach peak effectiveness. You might experience some side effects like a decrease in sex drive and weight gain, but we can keep an eye on that. If it becomes an issue, we can try something else."

I haven't had much of a sexual appetite in the last several months. Larry and I are both so busy that sex isn't something we do very often anyway. The weight gain concerns me a little. I've been losing and gaining the same fifty pounds for ten years, and I'm currently in a loss cycle.

Anxiety is the more immediate threat, so I'll take the Paxil. I've not forgotten that summer of panic attacks; it haunts me worse than Bruce dreams.

"Can I still take Xanax if I need to?" I ask, already strategizing a new source if she says no.

"Yes, but I think you'll start to feel a difference soon with the Paxil."

⊙ ⊙ ⊙

Within two weeks, I felt more normal. Now, six weeks in, I don't feel much of anything.

"So, have you thought more about seeing a therapist?" my doctor asks.

"Yes, and I will. It's just that my schedule is crazy right now."

I will put off therapy as long as possible because I know what's causing my anxiety: it's all the death talk and reminiscing. In time, it will work itself out. In time, I'll be fine.

Part Four

The Whole Bruce Thing

CHAPTER 28

2006

I found a picture of me sitting in my parents' family room holding weeks-old Carlene. It's dated May 1, 1983, a few days after I'd moved off the farm. Carlene is wearing a light-blue terry sleeper, lying frog-like on my chest and sleeping, her mouth frozen in a post-feeding pucker. I'm wearing a purple blouse and a short, thin gold necklace with a single pearl at the end. I'm looking down at her, and my profile reveals a slight double chin.

I don't remember that picture being taken, just as I don't remember the actual move. After I'd sorted, boxed up, and given or thrown away Bruce's things, it's like I went to sleep and woke up in a new apartment.

For more than half of my adult life, I've told the same pithy story:

"My husband died when I was nineteen."

Pause.

"In a train wreck."

Pause.

"And our baby was eleven days old."

The last part is always the kicker. People respond with shock, followed by expressions of sympathy.

I usually shrug and say, "I got through it; I'm fine!"

When I tell this to my therapist, Amy, during our first session, she says that denial is one way in which I protect myself from the trauma of Bruce's death.

Trauma. Not a word I've considered to describe my grief experience.

"Your symptoms are consistent with post-traumatic stress

disorder," she says, showing me the description in the *Diagnostic and Statistical Manual of Mental Disorders.*

"Hmmm. I don't think so," I say, like Bruce's death was nothing more than a broken leg. "That's something soldiers have, not someone whose husband died."

Amy explains that the part of the brain responsible for rational thought, the prefrontal cortex, isn't fully mature until age twenty-five. When I was nineteen, most of my thinking and decision-making was done in my amygdala, the emotion and fear center of the brain. How I formed my long-term memories of the accident and how I processed and didn't process what happened that day and the years after was also due to my immature prefrontal cortex. Add to the mix that I never saw Bruce's body and was denied a physical ending, the experience of his death was doubly traumatic.

I'm not averse to this diagnosis, although my now-mature prefrontal cortex thinks she's making a bigger deal of this than is necessary.

"How can something that happened twenty-three years ago still make me feel so anxious and angry?" I ask. "Shouldn't all of this emotional crap be gone by now?"

"I'm afraid time doesn't 'heal' anything," she says.

Ah, that's right. David warned me about that.

"Same time next week?" She writes on an appointment card.

There's a section of abandoned rail line that expands over the Clarion River and into a mountain tunnel. It's twenty degrees colder inside the mouth of the tunnel, but that's not what chills you. It's the wind that blows all around you, like ghosts flying out of the darkness. When Amy hands me the card, I feel those ghosts blowing around me.

I take the card and smile weakly. "I'll be here."

CHAPTER 29

No one has to dangle Xanax in front of me this time. I want to be in therapy, but not because I woke up one morning giddy to address my mental health.

In 2004—three years after Tony died, Carlene's project ended, and I went on Paxil—I weighed 300 pounds. Some of my weight gain was due to an undiagnosed thyroid issue, but much of it was a side effect of Paxil.

I wasn't happy, and I wasn't unhappy, but I rarely felt any emotion to an extreme. Paxil numbed most of my feelings, including those pertaining to my weight and body image. When we took a family trip to Niagara Falls, I ignored my knees as they ached and crunched. I ignored my ankles as they turned out when I walked a few blocks up Clifton Hill. The stabbing pain in my lower back and the sweat dripping between my breasts and down my spine? I ignored that, too. If I didn't fit in a seat at some event, I stood in the back or went home. When I broke my desk chair, I blamed faulty mechanics.

I lost interest in writing about people, and since writing about people was part of my job, I quit the newspaper and bought an antique store.

My interest in antiques started years ago when I bought a 1906 leatherbound edition of *The Mill on the Floss* at a flea market. I also started collecting vintage German porcelain, real photo postcards of Jasper, 3-D stereoviews, and nineteenth-century books on human sexuality. In antique stores, I lost myself in the stories of things, both regarding their function and who their previous owners were.

There was one store I especially enjoyed, located in a former general store in a small town twenty miles north of Clarion. Outside and inside, the two-story building was stuffed with every kind of antique and collectible imaginable, from buttons and scythes to dough bowls and dress forms. Built in 1892, the main room retained the smell of old wood and ash from the potbelly stove, and another room was filled floor to ceiling with hundreds of books arranged by topic on old maple library shelves.

While Paxil kept my emotions fairly anesthetized, what I felt when I was in that store was peaceful isolation. When my stepson Kevin was two years old, his first complete sentence was "Go away and leave me alone!" and that's what I could do in that store: go away and be left alone. When the owners mentioned that they were thinking of selling, I was obsessed with buying it, and I convinced myself, my dad (who loaned me the money for the down payment), and Larry (who reluctantly signed his name on the purchase agreement) that the store would make me happy.

At seventy-one, Dad wanted to retire from his sales job, but he needed something else to do every day, something with purpose. Our agreement when he loaned me the money was that he and Mom would move to Pennsylvania and live in the apartment above the store. He would work for me in exchange for rent. It was a sweet arrangement. Dad, who could talk to anyone *and enjoyed it*, would be my salesclerk, and I wouldn't have to interact, at least not much, with the public.

Dad thrived at the store. He turned the back room into a workshop and repaired items I bought at auctions for resale. In the spring and summer, he'd share his lunch on the front porch with our golden retriever, Jake, and talk to whomever happened by. During the winter, when we were closed, he made cribbage boards, candlesticks, and paper towel holders to sell at craft shows.

After a year, Mom found it difficult living in a remote area and in an apartment in which she had to descend and climb nineteen stairs every time she went somewhere. She and Dad bought a small house in Clarion, ending our rent-for-labor agreement. Dad still came to work every day, and I had to pay him a salary, but since I'd not yet had a profitable month, and I wasn't comfortable renting the apartment to strangers with so many valuable items downstairs, Larry and I sold our house in Clarion and moved to the store.

I thought I'd enjoy living without neighbors and the constant threat of someone stopping by the house to chat, but living in isolation wasn't the same as working in isolation. Days went by when I didn't step outside the store, and Dad and Larry were the only people I interacted with. I loved them both, but they didn't exactly constitute a social life. And those damn stairs. Every night, when I "came home" from work, I had to sit for five minutes to catch my breath.

Before it had become necessary to move to the apartment, Larry and I had put a deposit down on a cabin rental for a one-week vacation in the Adirondacks in late-September. After we moved, I wanted to cancel the trip and get our money back, but Larry insisted we go. He considered the Adirondacks, especially the high peaks, his spiritual home, and it had been years since we were there.

We stayed in a small wood cabin perched thirty feet from the Kiwassa Outlet of Saranac Lake. "Camp Helen" was etched on a board above the screened porch. The leaves were just starting to change, so the trees were still full enough to hide the cabins around us.

I was drinking coffee on the porch the first morning when Larry yelled up from the dock, "Let's go fishing!"

It would be a perfect day on the water. The lake was calm and not crowded, the temperature was comfortable, but I was feeling mildly anxious. It wasn't the first time in the last few months that I'd felt that way, and I suspected my Paxil tolerance was waning. I'd also experienced familiar negative thought patterns from my past: a longing to be small, not in a physical way but unnoticed, and the desire to take up as little space as possible, to not be a bother.

"Nah, you go!" I yelled back. "Catch us some dinner!"

I watched Larry step into the boat and row effortlessly out of sight. I wished I was with him. I wished I wanted it enough to try.

I walked down to the dock to read a book. A great blue heron was poised in the marsh on the opposite side of the bay. A few common mergansers floated by, and I heard, but couldn't see, some type of warbler. It was all so peaceful, yet the anxiety persisted. I could have taken Xanax, but I decided to ride out the feeling. I can't say why. It's not like I got brave all of a sudden. I just wasn't afraid of fear in that moment.

A few hours later, Larry returned with two small fish that he threw back in the lake.

"Let's go to Whiteface tomorrow," he said.

We'd planned to visit John Brown's family home near Lake Placid and go to the base of Mount Marcy and marvel at its magnificence, but driving up a 4,800-foot mountain wasn't on our agenda.

"I don't know." *Why is he asking me to do this? He knows I'm afraid of heights.* "If we do, I'm staying in the car."

"Are you sure? I'll hold your hand. We don't have to get close to the edge."

"Okay, maybe. If I get dizzy, you have to help me back to the car."

The next morning, driving up the winding road to the top of Whiteface—a jagged, 5-million-year-old mountain—I caught glimpses through the trees of how high we were climbing. Once we passed the tree line, the view was everywhere: blue-green mountains and sky as far as the eye could see.

You're safe in the car, you're safe in the car . . .

Larry parked in the lot near the summit. "Ready?"

"No," I said, but got out of the car anyway.

Near the visitor's center, a two-foot-high stone wall was all that separated us from falling to our death. From ten feet away, I glanced over the edge, and though my impulse was to back away, I walked a few feet closer.

"You can see Vermont over there," Larry said, pointing. "And those are the White Mountains in New Hampshire. And waaaay up there—can you see it? Maybe it's too hazy—is Montreal."

Larry wanted to walk up to the summit. I told him I'd meet him back at the car, but instead, I decided to wait on a bench outside the visitor's center. I watched people come and go, and I wondered what it felt like to be unaware or not care that we were seven-eighths of a mile in the air, among other things: *I used to love to fly. And I had dinner once at that restaurant on the fiftieth floor of the IDS building. Oh . . . what was its name? I worked at Musicland then, and that guy from the warehouse took me there, told me to order anything I wanted, but the prices, holy cow! The view was spectacular and—didn't he kiss me in the elevator? Jeez, I'm afraid of elevators now, too. When did that, how did that—*

"Wow!" Larry said, startling me. "That was amazing! Ready to head back?"

"I am. But would you take a photo of me in front of the elevation sign first?"

Larry's eyes shot up. He knew how much I hated having my photo taken. "Really?"

I handed him my camera. "Yeah, I don't know why, but something tells me I should preserve this moment. Proof that I was actually here."

I posed in mock terror. Larry took the photo and handed me my camera. Despite my disheveled hair, the flannel shirt around my waist, and my work boots, which I never tied, I didn't delete the photo.

⊙ ⊙ ⊙

A few weeks after we returned from the Adirondacks, our ten-year-old yellow lab began to struggle going up and down stairs, and she often urinated by the door, which seemed to embarrass her. When I took her to the animal clinic, the vet said that Sasha's diabetes and hip dysplasia was becoming unmanageable. Despite her wagging tail, Sasha was in a lot of pain, and the vet encouraged me to consider putting her down.

I called Larry on my way home.

"She thinks we need to do it this afternoon! What should we do?"

"I'll be right home," he said.

I waited for him on the deck, petting Sasha and crying into her thick neck.

When we'd adopted her, we already had two other large rescue dogs: Jake and a beagle mix named Mathilda. A friend had asked me to go to the Humane Society to help her pick out a dog for herself, and even though I was banned by my family from ever entering the shelter again, I agreed to go. Walking down the concrete row, dogs barking and fussing on either side of me, I spotted a six-year-old, stocky, broad-shouldered English yellow lab. When I stopped at her cage, she tried to hop, but her front feet barely left the ground. A staff member said she'd been in a shelter in Ohio for several weeks and had gotten so hoarse that she couldn't bark.

I brought her outside, and she stayed right beside me. I sat down on a bench, and she wagged her tail and licked my hands before sitting down, too. She looked skyward, with her eyes shut, like she was soaking in the sunshine.

I called Larry and asked him to come out to the shelter, but I didn't tell him why because he would have hung up on me.

"Shelly wants your opinion on a dog," I lied.

I could tell by the look on his face that he was *not* happy when he pulled into the parking lot and saw me with the lab. He didn't say a word, but to his credit, he looked her over and walked her a little.

"Can we talk about it?" he asked.

We went home. We talked. Two hours later, she was ours.

Sasha was fully trained, she heeled, she listened, she didn't chew furniture or shoes, and she slept sixteen hours a day. Her only beef was with Mathilda, whom I'd named after my great-grandmother. When Mathilda got too close, Sasha would let out a strange *Exorcist*-like growl and look sideways at her with wild eyes. We always expected her head to start spinning.

The night before Sasha was diagnosed with diabetes, I'd slept with her on the living room floor because she was too weak to climb the stairs to our bedroom. The next day, after the vet gave me a script for insulin, I brought it to our drugstore. The pharmacy tech said I could pick it up in a few hours. From there, I would take Sasha back to the clinic to learn how to administer the shot.

When I returned to the drugstore, the tech who'd helped me earlier was waiting on someone else, and the pharmacist, perched above me and staring at a computer screen, said they wouldn't have the insulin for at least a day.

"But you said you had it!" I yelled, surprising everyone, including me. The pharmacist's eyes remained glued to the computer screen. "Maybe she's just a dog to you, but she's my friend, and she'll die without medicine!"

The only sound in the entire store was Muzak and me crying. The pharmacist didn't say a word. I turned around and stormed out.

The phone was ringing when I walked in the house. It was the tech from the pharmacy.

"I called around, and Walmart has the insulin," she said. "It will be ready in an hour."

"Oh, thank you! Thank you so much! I'm sorry I got so upset."

"It's okay. I have a dog, too."

Not long after that, Sasha was back to her happy self, loving everyone and hating Mathilda.

Now we only had a few hours left. Larry and I brought Sasha to my parents' house so they could say goodbye, too. We fed her all her favorite foods that she hadn't been allowed to eat for the past two years: peanut butter, ice cream, Milk Bones, and Greenies. Blind from cataracts, her gray-white eyes still sparkled in anticipation of each treat. She grunted as she ate, and her large tail slammed the ground in rhythm to her chewing.

When we arrived at the clinic, we were led to "the room" that every pet owner dreads.

"How are we supposed to say goodbye?" I whispered.

Larry shrugged and wiped his eyes.

We sat on the floor and petted Sasha until her eyes closed and her breathing stopped.

When we got home, tired and aching with grief, Larry poured us each a drink, and we sat down on the couch. Jake and Mathilda sensed something was wrong, and they laid quietly on the floor by our feet. We talked about how we did the right thing, like that was supposed to make us feel better, but her absence weighed heavy.

I decided a few days later that my sadness was overkill and that I was overreacting to something I knew was inevitable. I threw out Sasha's toys and washed and packed away her bed. A week after we picked up the urn with her remains, we adopted another dog, an eight-month-old flat-coated retriever we named Cooper, who proved to be an apt distraction from missing Sasha, although the mention of her name still made me sad.

⊙ ⊙ ⊙

A few months later, on Cassie's twentieth birthday, I offered to cook one of her favorite meals, but she insisted we go out to one of her favorite restaurants.

"It's snowing," I said.

"Mom!" she said, like a finger snap.

Getting ready to go, I pulled my hair back in a ponytail. My haircut was uneven, and the color was a combination of store-bought blonde, dark roots, and strands of gray. I'd stopped going to the salon because sitting in the chair was as uncomfortable as staring at my reflection in the mirror. I trimmed my bangs when they grew past my eyes, and I lopped off the ends in the back when they looked frayed.

I put on a stretchy red sweater over my stretchy black pants with the small hole and a permanent stain on the leg. Not much fit anymore, and I didn't have the money to upgrade my wardrobe another size.

"You look nice," said Larry. He kissed my cheek before putting on his coat.

"Whatever."

We met Cassie and Carlene at the restaurant, and despite the weather, the place was filled with preholiday parties. We were seated next to a window with a stunning view of the snow falling on the Allegheny River.

The girls were animated, as usual, talking over each other and carrying on two conversations at once. Listening to them was one of the few things that always made me happy.

I knew it was futile to say no to a photo when Cassie handed her camera to Larry and said, "Take a picture of me and Mom!"

"Smile!" he said, and I did.

"That's a nice photo of us!" Cassie said, showing it to me.

I agreed because I couldn't tell her what I really thought. Then I looked at the photo more closely. Cassie had placed her cheek next to mine, and she was beaming. She was happy because she was with her mother on her birthday. Not her ill-dressed, isolated, self-loathing mother. Cassie and Carlene loved me. All of me.

"I love this," I said. "Send me a copy."

◉ ◉ ◉

After starting Paxil, I'd stopped paying attention when my doctor talked about my weight and its connection to my high blood pressure and high cholesterol, but during an appointment a week after Cassie's birthday, my ears perked up when she added that I was prediabetic.

"All of this can lower your life expectancy," she warned.

I hadn't thought about my death the same as I did the death of others. Since Bruce died, I'd been afraid of being left again, afraid of that heart-wrenching, soul-sucking grief. Now I had to consider how my death would inflict the same pain on the people I loved, especially my kids.

On January 1, 2005, I started eating less. That was it, just a small change that I didn't tell anyone about. When I saw my doctor again in February, I'd had lost fifteen pounds, and I felt strangely positive for the first time in years. I was engaging change instead of passively allowing change to happen.

Never one to sit with a feeling and let it marinate, though, I jumped onto the next change.

"I want to stop taking Paxil," I told my doctor.

"Are you sure? The withdrawal can be difficult. Do you think you're ready?"

"Yes, I'm sure," I said with the confidence of someone who always thinks she knows what she's doing.

"Okay, but it will take some time. Maybe five or six months." She wrote a script for a dose just a few milligrams less than my current dose. "Take this for two weeks. After that, cut those tabs in half for two more weeks. Call me if you have any problems. I want to see you again in four weeks."

Things went smoothly at first. I could feel the brain fog lifting. I wanted to engage people again. I even went to a party and didn't feel anxious.

Things got real a month later when my doctor cut my dose in half again. I was dizzy much of the time, and my nerves were on fire. Anger became a dominant emotion. When I told her my symptoms, my doctor upped the dose by a few milligrams and said I'd need to slow down the withdrawal to let my body adjust.

Journal entry, May 1, 2005: At the risk of killing someone, I have to go even slower! I want off this damn stuff now! I'm exercising like a maniac to get rid of the hundred fucking pounds I gained since going on this fucking drug. I can't even tell you what the last four years have really felt like. I hate everyone, or at least everyone bugs the shit out of me to some point. I've never felt so out of my body before. Raging, crying, raging, crying. I'm exhausted.

I was cold all the time.
I couldn't stop moving.

I developed a weird sensation on the balls of my feet, like a feather brushing over them.

I developed a heightened sensitivity to pain and light.

I hated the smell of air.

I didn't ask for support from or offer support to Larry, who was named chair of the chemistry department following the death of a colleague who was serving as chair.

I rationed compassion—toward myself and others—like it was nylons during World War II.

I was irrational and thoughtless.

Most of all, I was scared. I'd never hated anyone more than I hated myself.

◎ ◎ ◎

It happened at almost every auction. I would find one thing I wanted in a box lot, maybe a piece of vintage cast iron or an intact *Dick and Jane*, but my winning bid meant I had to take home the entire contents, things like black-encrusted frying pans, warped Popsicle molds, and metal ice trays missing the dividers. Every few months, Dad and I took the discarded stuff to an auction house that sold it for me, and while I didn't net much cash, it cleared out the storage room for the next round of box-lot junk.

It was during our auction house trip in October when Dad dropped the news: Mom wanted to move back to Minnesota.

My parents, at least as long as I'd known them, were grass-is-always-greener types. Every time they moved (with or without kids), Dad said it was because they had "itchy moving feet." That's why what he said about returning to Minnesota didn't surprise me, but I was pretty sure Dad wasn't the one with itchy feet this time.

In August, Mom and I had gone out for lunch, and as soon as we sat down, I could tell Mom was in a mood.

I mentioned the phone call I received the night before from mutual friends in Canada. They called me every year on my birthday.

"I email them, and I never hear from them, so I just give up," Mom said.

"Do you check your spam file?" I asked. "Maybe they've replied and it's gone there?"

Mom ordered another glass of wine and waved away my question.

I said that Larry's birthday gift to me was tickets to a concert in Cleveland the next weekend.

"Dad and I won't be going anywhere this year," Mom said.

Somehow that was my fault, I was certain.

After we ate, the restaurant grew dark, and I checked the weather app on my phone.

"I have to go," I said. "I left the windows in the sunporch open."

"Oh, well, I heard something different, I guess," Mom said. "There's just a chance of rain."

I'd heard versions of these snipes all my life, and they always landed in my brain as, "Fix it, Lynn!" I couldn't change the weather, but I felt guilty leaving, so I stayed until Mom was ready to leave, a glass of wine later.

I looked over at Dad and wondered if I was the reason Mom wanted to leave Pennsylvania. Twice she'd asked me to go to lunch since August, and both times I came up with an excuse rather than tell her the truth, that I was tired of the two-hour bitch sessions.

"Did she say why she needs to go back?" I asked.

"Well, she said she misses her sister . . ."

"Which one? She hardly saw any of them when you lived there."

"Yeah, but . . ."

I didn't press him. If Mom blamed me for wanting to move, Dad wouldn't tell me. Besides, there was nothing I could or would do about it anyway. Once Mom set something in motion, there was no changing her mind.

"You know what I realized this summer?" I said. "Nothing anyone says or does, or doesn't say or do, is ever enough. Mom can never be happy."

"Oh, I know that." Dad laughed. "But I have to try."

"How about Mom goes back to Minnesota and you stay?"

He smiled and shook his head no. "You know I can't do that."

Our annual pre-Christmas open house weekend was coming up in a few weeks. For three years, Mom had been in charge of the food table, and during those weekends, she was everything I wished she could be all the time: at ease around people and enjoying her life.

"I'll bet anything that one day she'll say, 'I wish we'd stayed in Pennsylvania,'" I said.

"Oh, I'm sure she will, too."

I reached over and took his hand. Dad was the lifeblood of the store. Many returning customers said they came back because of the fellow who looks like Santa. He knew every inch of the place: the side room filled with glass insulators, wooden rakes, tin mailboxes, and other random rusty things, and the creepy basement with its stone walls that leaked every time it rained. Each change of season, he helped me wash and redecorate the large bay windows that bookended the front door.

"I can't run the place without you."

"I know," he said. "I'm sorry, honey."

I squeezed his hand. "No, Dad, I'm sorry. I really do understand, and it'll be okay. Everything'll be okay."

⊙ ⊙ ⊙

On November 10, nine months after I started tapering, I took my last dose of Paxil. Three weeks later, I still experienced occasional nerve zaps and bouts of chills. Anger, while at a more palatable level, was still all too present. An overarching fear of fear emerged like thirteen-year cicadas, and I considered running back to Paxil like I was its estranged lover and beg it to take me back into its numbing arms.

The night before I called my doctor to let her know I wanted to take Paxil again, I reread my journal entries from the last five months. Every day, every minute, had held a different emotion or physical sensation. I'd volleyed anger with over-the-top joy, confusion with certainty, defeat with success, and now, I was so close to being free, did I really want to go back?

I journaled about Dr. Angry and his theory about grief being the root cause of . . . well . . . everything, and I counted back the number of years since I'd last seen him—nineteen, the same age I was when Bruce died.

Journal entry, November 30, 2005: "It's time I dealt with the whole Bruce thing."

CHAPTER 30

Today in our session, Amy asks what I remember about anger as a child.

I tell her how Mom had sole ownership of it in our home, and how, for the rest of us, it was a one-way emotion. She encouraged our anger if it was aimed at others, but she—and by extension, Dad—never taught us how to express it in a constructive way. All I knew about anger was that after you yelled and slammed cupboards and bedroom doors, you left.

"Now that I think about it, it was so ridiculous," I say, reaching for a tissue.

I feel uncomfortable tattling on my mother this way, but I can't stop. It's like I'm on a sled, sailing down an icy hill toward a tree.

"I must have done something wrong. I don't know what. 'Go play in the sandbox!' she said and locked the door."

"How old were you?"

"Five? I think? I told my older sister about it a few years ago, and she said that Mom would sometimes meet her at the door when she got home from grade school and make her take me for walks, even in winter."

My palms are sweating, and I can feel my heartbeat in my ears as I throw my mother under the bus. Even though she and Dad moved back to Minnesota a month ago, I just know she knows I'm talking about her. I have to fix it.

"Mom had a rough childhood. She was the fifth of five girls, and her father was mad that she wasn't a boy. She's not a bad person. I mean, I know she loves me!"

"I'm sure she does," Amy says. "But it's important to understand how her anger impacts you."

It does, I admit, and what I learned about anger impacts my kids, too. Once, when Christopher and I were separated, we had a screaming match over the phone. When I hung up, I slammed the phone so hard and so many times that it shattered the receiver. Carlene, who was nine, and Cassie, seven, were listening and watching from the living room. Carlene walked up to me and said, "Mama, it scares me when you yell. Cassie, too."

I reach for another tissue. "I was horrified and so embarrassed! How could I do that to my kids?"

"Would you have been able to say to your mom what your daughter said to you?" Amy asks.

"Ha! No!"

Amy says that Carlene must have been confident that I wouldn't retaliate when she told me how she felt, and that she wasn't afraid that I would walk away and ignore her. While Amy's explanation doesn't make me feel much better about my actions, she adds that I should give myself credit for recognizing how my anger impacts others.

Next, she asks if I was ever angry at Bruce. Unlike when Dr. Angry asked the same question, I don't feel judged, and I tell her about the argument after the miscarriage.

"I was angry, sure, but I was more disappointed than anything. Bruce never had my back when it came to his father. He would say the most cutting things, and Bruce would say nothing."

For a moment, I feel like I'm throwing Bruce under the bus, too, the man I've canonized as a saint, but I keep going.

"I know Bruce hated conflict, but his silence hurt."

I think how therapy this time is like a thousand-piece puzzle. Amy and I have framed the outside, and now we're working on connecting the inside pieces. When I remember something that seems random, I've learned to trust that it's okay to verbalize it. We'll sort out if that piece fits anywhere in the puzzle we're working on or if it's the missing piece to a different one.

"At breakfast the morning he died, I asked Bruce if he would go with me to Pipestone after lunch to go grocery shopping and buy a bottle of champagne for our anniversary. I told him I wanted to spend some time alone with him while my mom was still there. He said that would be fun, or something like that, and asked me to leave a check for my mom to give the fuel guy. 'There's still plenty of winter left, so I called to have the oil tank filled this afternoon,' he said. Why do I remember that? Anyway, just before he went outside, he said he'd be in at noon. God, it was all so . . . ordinary. And then, of course, I never saw him again."

I take a moment to breathe. I want to say what I'm thinking in the most coherent way I can.

"Sometimes I wonder why he went to town that morning without telling me first. I mean, if he was too busy to go to Pipestone and thought he had to get all his work done before we left, he didn't have to go with me. But was he afraid to tell me that? Was he afraid I'd get angry?"

More silence.

"Is that why I have a really hard time asking someone to do something for me? They'll die because I'm selfish, because I need or want to be with them?"

Amy writes a few notes, then looks at me thoughtfully. I'm not sure if I'm ready to say the rest of what's in my head, what's always been in my head.

"I was pretty mad at him when he died. Saying that feels really shitty."

Amy assures me, like Dr. Angry tried to, that anger is a common reaction when someone dies. Logically, I know it's not my fault that Bruce died. But I'm still not sure it wasn't his fault that he died, either. *How do you not hear a train?* I can't get that question out of my head, but I keep that one to myself.

"Don't forget the cushion," she says as our session ends.

When we first met, Amy had introduced me to the writings and recordings of Buddhist psychologists Jon Kabat-Zinn and Tara Brach. I found their meditation techniques similar to Herbert Benson's Relaxation Response, which I hadn't practiced in twenty years. Sitting and breathing and bringing my wandering mind back to the moment was nearly impossible at first, but I'm up to ten minutes now, and afterward, I always feel calmer. It's remembering to sit and breathe that is my struggle.

She hands me another CD of a Tara Brach meditation. "Same time next week?"

I am drained, I feel guilt and regret, and my stomach is a twisted knot.

"Thank you, yes. See you then."

CHAPTER 31

"When I saw his name on the called ID, my heart skid to the edge of a panic attack," I tell Amy. "'Call me back, damn it!' was his first message."

Cassie is getting married in a few months, and because RJ is her legal father, she'd called him regarding a few questions that were on the marriage license. When he didn't answer, she'd left him a message. Rather than call her back, he'd called me.

"A few minutes later, he called and left another message, yelling about how invasive the questions were and that it was no one's damn business and on and on. I was shaking so bad, I thought I was going to throw up."

Amy assures me that's a classic PTSD response.

Like grief, I thought my fear of RJ would go away over time. But the lingering trauma from his past violence and verbal threats had roared back the minute I'd heard his voice.

I tell Amy about the last time I'd witnessed his violence. It was after the divorce, on one of his custody weekends. Carlene was visiting Walt and Eileen, so Cassie was at his place alone. Cassie is outgoing and loves being the center of attention, but I knew she missed her sister, so I called RJ to check how she was doing by herself. When he answered, he slurred his words as he told me to never call the kids on his weekend.

Disgusted but not surprised, I told him I was taking her home.

"Don't you . . ." he started to say before I hung up.

When I knocked on his apartment door, RJ yelled that he was calling the police.

"Go ahead!" I yelled back. "If that's how I have to get my kid out of there, do it!"

His fiancé was with him, and she convinced him to open the door.

"Get Cassie!" I demanded.

"She's sleeping!"

"I don't care. I'm taking her home!"

RJ stormed into Cassie's room, grabbed her out of bed, and threw her into the hallway.

"Take the little shit! I never want to see her again!"

Cassie looked over at me and started to cry. I ran down the hall and gathered her in my arms.

"Asshole," I said, walking out the door.

"Bitch!" he yelled.

"Cass slept with me that night. She was so afraid. Hell, I was afraid! She wasn't even five years old! Who does that to a little kid!" I tell Amy, but what I'm thinking is, *Who let's that happen to a little kid? Why didn't I do more?*

I say how I'd kept them away from him as much as I could, but because I couldn't prove he'd been violent, he threatened to sue me if I didn't allow him visitation.

"Mostly, though, I didn't want to believe what was happening."

Amy says that trauma can paralyze us because it's too painful otherwise.

"Still, I should have stood up for them more. Bruce would've have been so disappointed in me, allowing his daughter to be raised by that jerk."

"You don't think he would have been concerned instead?"

Maybe, but I feel like I'm always letting him down. I've made so many stupid decisions since he died.

⊙ ⊙ ⊙

Before our next session, I drive down to the Clarion River to think. My mind has been swimming all week, butterfly style.

Stroke after stroke, I push forward in time, from Bruce to RJ, to college, to meeting Christopher, to marrying Christopher, to divorcing Christopher.

I think about how happy I was in college, and how my intellectual confidence grew exponentially, driven largely by Christopher's encouragement. At the same time, I was on guard for the next RJ incident. I denied it then, but I'd married Christopher to get away from RJ, and because I wasn't honest with myself, because I ignored what I knew deep down was true, I did something that hurt Christopher and eventually the girls, who'd grown to love him like a father.

I slip in the CD *Our Time in Eden* by 10,000 Maniacs and play "Jezebel," a self-flagellating song that helps me feel appropriately awful about myself.

A few days after Christopher and I separated, he'd stopped by our house to pick up more of his things. He thought I was at work, but I was upstairs.

I heard footsteps on the porch and flew down the stairs in time to see Christopher staring at another man's shoes on the rug.

Christopher looked at me blankly. Then, without a word, he turned and walked out the door.

Nothing could justify the way I cheated and lied myself out of our relationship, a relationship Christopher trusted me with and believed in. Nothing could excuse why I didn't let go of us when I realized I didn't love him.

"I've created so much chaos in my life," I say in our next session. "I'm erratic and irresponsible. Rootless. A flake."

"You own the consequences of your choices, right?" Amy asks.

I nod.

"And can you forgive yourself?"

I think about this for a minute. I'd perpetrated some pretty deep pain and had apologized to Christopher many times, but there's more to the Christopher story, more I need to process before I can answer her question.

I tell her that, like RJ, Christopher isn't talking to the girls and hasn't for seven years. When Carlene and Cassie were in high school, Christopher wanted to take them on their yearly week-long vacation to the beach, only that year he booked a house for the week before the end of school. Cassie was barely passing two of her classes, and I didn't want her to miss any school right before finals, so I said he couldn't take them on vacation at that time. We argued. He called me controlling. I called him unreasonable. Both were true.

While Christopher was not legally obligated to them, he'd been giving me $100 a month to help pay for some of their essentials. After the fight, he emailed me and said he was stopping the monthly stipend to "punish" me.

Part of me thought he was treating me like a child, and part of me thought I deserved it after what I did to him when we were married. Maybe I shouldn't have, but I told the kids about Christopher's email, which made them mad, not because of the money but because of the whole "punishing" me thing.

Carlene has my temper, unfortunately, and she stopped going over to Christopher's house. When he wrote her an email a few months later to tell her that he and his girlfriend had a birthday gift for her and asked her to come get it, she wrote back and said she didn't want it. He wrote back and called her a bitch and a spoiled brat. Cassie, in support of her sister, stopped going to his house, too, and that was the end of their relationship with Christopher.

"I should have handled all of it better than I did, and I still feel like it's my fault that he's not talking to them . . ."

I stop. I heard what I just said: "I should have" and "my fault." I see a pattern emerge. My mom, Bruce, RJ, Christopher, and others. I apologize for things that aren't mine to apologize for, and fix, or at least think it's my responsibility to fix, broken things that I didn't break.

"Wait a minute," I continue. "The girls were sixteen and fourteen. Christopher was a grown-ass man. Could I have handled that whole situation better? Yes. But he could have made an effort to make it better, too. I'm willing to own my part in this, my anger and all that, but I can't own Christopher's anger, too. So, yes, I think I can forgive myself. But from now on, how do I hand other people's behavior back to them and say, 'This belongs to you'?"

Amy smiles. "That's a really good question. How do you think you should answer it?"

I'm not sure, but I'm face-to-face with a shadow issue that has been lurking for years, and I won't run from it. Not this time.

◉ ◉ ◉

If old buildings and antiques have taught me anything, it's that when you take up carpet on wood floors or strip the paint off an old cabinet, it usually takes a good amount of effort to restore whatever's underneath. It's not easy acknowledging the pain I've caused others and the ways and reasons for why I run away, but as the weeks pass, therapy feels less confessional and more focused on understanding "why." I'm slowly loosening my grip on guilt and accepting that, while cause isn't an excuse, it's possible to be culpable without drowning in blame. I'm recognizing when grief, anger, and anxiety are separate experiences and when they are intertwined.

I also feel purposeful again and doing what I feel meant to do. Write.

The first time my name was published in a newspaper was in 1992. I'd been so steaming mad after listening to vice president Quayle verbally attack the fictional television character, Murphy

Brown, for being a single mother that I fired off a letter to the editor. I didn't stop to consider how my words might be construed by detractors or that I might have supporters. I just sealed the envelope and dropped it in the mail.

The paper published my letter, and three days later, I received a note from the president of the local domestic violence agency. She had read my letter to the editor and asked if I would consider joining their board of directors.

My letter to the editor had opened doors I never would have knocked on. It taught me how my words could affect change and how, unlike a private journal, published words can create a conversation with people I might not otherwise talk to. When I was offered the opportunity to start my own column at the *Clarion News*, I used that space to write about universal themes and to help me make sense of my political and social ideology, and I engaged in conversations with a broad readership.

In my final column in April 2002, I told readers that I would never be back, and at the time, I meant it. Paxil had quieted my need to write and have conversations with others. When I was six months Paxil-free, I called Rodney and told him I wanted to write again.

"Welcome back, babe!" he said.

Last week, in my resurrected column, I pedaled back the words I wrote four years earlier: "In the 187 weeks since the last time you saw my name in this space, I've learned the gravity of the word 'never.' I will never again silence my voice, and listening to it will be my never-ending pursuit."

I miss the store, though. When Mom and Dad moved back to Minnesota, I sold the building and auctioned the contents, and Larry and I moved back to Clarion. I miss the ghosts that padded up the side stairs in the book room and left items askew on shelves. I miss the thrill of turning off the last light when closing for the day and wondering if they'd follow me up the stairs. I miss it mostly because the new owner tore down my peaceful, hardworking store and paved over it.

I refuse to see it gone. Like Bruce, I need it to remain alive in my mind, although remembering details about Bruce is difficult. The more I understand grief and its vagabond temperament—here one moment, gone the next, never knowing when it will show up again—the more I lose sight of him. I can't remember what his face felt like against mine when we danced, what his breath felt and tasted like when he kissed me, how he held my waist in his hands. I can't even remember what kind of underwear he wore or what type of socks he preferred or what his favorite cologne smelled like.

It's like he's been paved over.

I'd asked my dad once how he was able to remember so much about his father, especially since Dad was so young. He said that he'd made a conscious decision, as soon as he was told his father was dead, to memorize everything he could, including his first taste of his father's horseradish that he helped him make when he was only two years old.

"Sometimes it's the smallest thing that will trigger a memory," he said.

This morning, sitting in my car in the dark at the gym, waiting for the rain to let up, "The First Time Ever I Saw Your Face" came on the radio, and a small detail emerged, unfolding like a crocus on a spring morning.

I remembered Bruce's soft brown chest hair.

I searched the car for paper, anything, to write it down. I dug out my checkbook and ripped out four deposit slips: "I loved to touch his chest lightly, run my fingers across his muscles—he was so strong—and rest my head just below his shoulder. We'd lie on our bed and talk and listen to music for hours.

"I remember watching him drum the steering wheel to his favorite songs. I remember listening to 'Young Turks' by Rod

Stewart in the tractor driving home from his brother's. What were the words? Something about life being short and doing all you can in the moment. That's true. I remember walking through the pasture on a Sunday afternoon and making love in the grass . . . God, we both felt so alive!"

The song ended and I stopped writing. I blew my nose in a Subway napkin I dug out of the glove box.

I miss him. I still love him. And thanks to therapy, I know that it's okay that I feel both.

CHAPTER 32

"Is it really a vacation if we visit family?" I ask Larry as we pack up the car.

"Maybe not that part," he says. "But we're stopping in Memphis, so that kind of counts as vacation."

We're leaving for Arkansas in the morning to spend Thanksgiving weekend with my Uncle David and Aunt Shirley, as well as Larry's sister and brother-in-law, all of whom live within ten minutes of each other in Bella Vista. We will also visit Larry's mother, who has advanced Alzheimer's and is living in a nursing facility in Bentonville.

I look forward to seeing everyone and seeing Memphis, although I know this vacation/family visit will challenge several of my resurrected post-Paxil fears.

"Don't forget to pack your cushion," Amy had said when we talked about coping strategies for when I felt overly anxious.

"I won't," I'd assured her. "I'm taking my Zen bag along, too."

Soon after I'd started therapy, I bought a pink backpack in which I keep a portable CD player, meditation CDs, and Jon Kabat-Zinn's book, *Wherever You Go, There You Are*. It's dogeared and waterlogged from when I dropped it in the bathtub, and I've written notes throughout the margins and highlighted copiously. The book has become as much a comfort as the teddy bear I've taken with me on every trip since high school.

"There are so many mountains and rivers between Pennsylvania and Arkansas!" I'd whined when Larry and I mapped out the drive. But I wanted to see those mountains and rivers, including the New River Gorge in West Virginia, which meant, Larry reminded me, that we'd have to drive across the 876-foot-high New River Gorge Bridge.

"Correction," I'd said. "*You* will have to drive across the New River Gorge Bridge. I'll be in the back seat with my eyes shut."

While they are part of the same mountain chain that runs through western Pennsylvania, the Allegheny Mountains in West Virginia are more imposing than the smaller hills around Clarion, and they loom over an equally intimidating freeway that twists, turns, rises, and falls like a Stephen King novel.

We spend the first night of our three-day drive in Bristol, Virginia, the furthest from home I've been since our vacation in the Adirondacks and the furthest south I've ever been. I feel a little anxious as we check into the hotel but remind myself that I always feel road buzzy after a long drive.

"Do you mind getting us some takeout?" I ask Larry after we're settled in our room. "I need to be quiet for a few minutes."

I can't eat when I'm nervous, but I plan to not be nervous by the time Larry returns with our food. I sit on the bed, shut my eyes, and do a body scan. My breath is shallow, and my muscles are tense. I open one eye, look over at my purse, and consider medicating over meditating.

"Don't be afraid to take it if you need to," Amy always tells me. "But give 'the cushion' five minutes first."

In the ten years between my divorce from RJ and the start of Carlene's senior project, I took very little Xanax, usually only needing it before a dentist appointment or flying, but I kept one with me at all times. Just knowing it was there, that I had a choice to take it or not, was usually enough to keep mild anxiety in check. I don't know if that trick will still work, but I close my eyes and give meditation a few more minutes. When I hear Larry's card slide in the lock and the door open a few minutes later, I am calm and hungry.

Back on the road the next morning, I see a sign for Cumberland Gap National Park.

"Oh, my gosh! I read about the Cumberland Gap when I was a kid!"

Larry looks at me and laughs. "How old are you?"

"I'm serious! I'm excited! There was a book we read in fifth grade about a family that went on vacation. They drove coast to coast in their station wagon, and we made a paper-mâché topographical map of their trip. I did the Cumberland Gap, and now, here I am, in the Cumberland Gap!"

I stare out at the Great Smoky Mountains and see . . . mountains. Not scary mountains, not intimidating mountains, just beautiful tree-topped mountains.

Examining anxiety in a detached and clinical way has been like turning on a light to see what's in that dark room that causes my anxiety, which I understand now to be a biproduct of trauma. Amy urges me to stay in the present and not project the future, both on and off the cushion, since the future is where anxiety lives. No matter how much I want to control the future and not be surprised by it, she reminds me that I can't know when someone will die or if I'll experience additional trauma. But I do have a choice. I can turn off the light and live in the dark, or I can allow the future to unfold, as it will do anyway without my help.

Keeping that light on isn't easy, but at least I know what I'm up against.

After spending a day and night in Memphis, I talk to my anxiety as I drive over the Mississippi River on the Memphis-Arkansas Bridge.

I see you, and, yes, you scare me a little, but that's it. That's all you get right now.

Greeted on the other side by the Arkansas delta, I am

surprised by how flat the land is. It looks like southwest Minnesota, only instead of cornfields, rice fields lie adjacent to the road.

"When was the last time I was in Minnesota?" I ask Larry.

He looks up from his book. "I don't know. Your dad's birthday, maybe?"

"Yeah, but I meant Jasper."

"It was before I knew you," he says and goes back to his book.

I run the years through my head. A minute later, I snap my fingers. "Grandma Signe's funeral. That's it."

Signe died, fittingly, on Leap Day 1996. When asked, I'd agreed to give her eulogy. With the amount of material I had to work with, it would practically write itself.

Among other memorable things, Grandma had an Andy Warhol eye for color (her costume jewelry always matched her pantsuits), and she owned a boat-sized green Chevy, which she drove with her right foot on the gas and her left foot on the brake.

The only thing that had concerned me about giving the eulogy was that memories of my former church—from childhood to widowhood—might click through my mind like a View-Master disc, and they'd either distract me or, worse, cause a panic attack. I hadn't had one in years, but I still lived in fear of them.

While I'd been inside the Lutheran church several times since Bruce died, I hadn't been in the funeral home and had no intention of attending Grandma's visitation. My little sister, however, had tagged along on the drive to Jasper, and she *wanted* to see Grandma laid out, so I got her there in time and decided I would hang out in the back.

Candle smoke and carnations—the smell of grief—hit my nose the second we walked in the door. Uncle David and Aunt Shirley were visiting with a few other people near the guest book. When she saw us, Shirley greeted us and said that Mom and Dad had left a few minutes earlier to check into their hotel. Then, almost singing the words, she said, "Let's go see Grandma!"

I understand the emotional and psychological importance of seeing a loved one dead, but I hadn't had a lot of practice. I was also pretty sure my grandmother wouldn't haunt my dreams like Bruce did, so I was alright with not seeing her.

"I really don't—" I edged toward the door.

"I know, Lynnie," Shirley said, drawing me to her. "But you need to say goodbye."

From the back of the room, I could see Signe's casket set in the same place as Bruce's thirteen years earlier, only hers was open. I saw the silhouette of her face and upper torso surrounded by plush cream fabric.

Shirley looped her arm through mine, and we walked down the aisle. I looked at the empty chairs to my right and thought, *Walt sat there. I held his hand. He thanked me for Carlene. He said he was sorry.*

At the casket, I looked around at everything except my grandmother: sprays of flowers set on easels, recessed lighting that spotlighted the area around the casket as though a play was about to begin, and the doorway to the room where the mortician . . . I shuddered thinking about what he did back there.

I didn't realize I was bouncing in my shoes until Shirley patted my hand and whispered, "You'll be fine."

I looked down at Signe. Her skin looked the same as when she was alive, snow-white and soft as flour, and her lips were positioned in a knowing smile. Her short gray curls were set as though she'd just walked out of the beauty parlor. Dementia had claimed her short-term memory in recent years, and in the nursing home, she often talked to her long-dead husband and asked staff and family when her mother and father were coming to visit. But that's not who I saw. The woman in the casket was the kind, fun, and sometimes bossy woman I loved.

"Goodbye, Grandma," I whispered, and then I turned to Shirley. "Thank you. I'm ready to go now."

⊙ ⊙ ⊙

In college, I'd learned a technique to practice before giving a presentation that helped reduce the chance of stage fright, and I decided to try it in my hotel room. I propped myself up against the headboard, shut my eyes, and visualized standing in the pulpit, where I'd give the eulogy, and looking out at the congregation. I allowed myself to remember as much as I could, from sitting with my family on Sunday mornings to singing in the children's choir to walking down the aisle . . . both times. I admire the thirty-foot peaked ceiling and the ten-foot, Gothic-arched stained glass windows on the outside walls. I can feel the hardness of the pews, smell the old wood embedded with years of candle smoke, and hear the organ and the preachers and the voices of bored children and crying babies and their parents trying desperately to keep them quiet.

I see Bruce in the choir loft, smiling at me.

I woke up a few hours later, unsure where I was. Papers were strung across the bed, and I remembered the eulogy. I placed the pages in order and read through them one last time before turning out the light. I would visit it again in the morning over breakfast. After that, I'd live with whatever came out of my mouth.

⊙ ⊙ ⊙

Although Signe was ninety-four when she died, and most of her friends and older family members were gone, the church was nearly full. Standing in the pulpit, staring out at the congregation, I remembered something else I'd learned in speech class: avoid looking at vulnerable people, those who might make you trip up your words with their nonverbal responses. If Dad or Uncle David cried, I'd cry, so I picked out two people near the back and talked at them.

A few minutes in, I was less nervous than I expected to be and decided to conclude with a small story that I'd given myself permission to skip if I was bombing.

"Signe was a first-rate knitter and doily maker. She made slippers for all of us, including my late husband, Bruce," I said, remembering to smile. "They were warm but really slippery, so you had to be careful walking on bare floors. She gave Bruce a pair for Christmas the year before he died, and he wore them every night when he came in from chores. He's buried in those slippers. When I'd told Signe, she said nothing. She was always quiet about death, but I know she loved and missed Bruce, and just like I miss him, I miss my grandma, too."

Because this was a Lutheran church, I didn't expect applause, but gauging by the smiles I received as I walked back to my seat, I probably did alright.

Lunch was served, like always, in the brightly lit social hall that still smelled of waxed floors and Folgers. I went through the serving line prepared by the Ladies Aid and placed a sandwich and a scoop of Jell-O salad on my plate. I chose a seat across from my former piano instructor and Bruce's sixth-grade teacher, and as we talked, others stopped by to tell me they enjoyed the eulogy.

I relished the feeling of being known, especially in that church. But while I felt more at home in Jasper than anywhere else, Jasper was also the epicenter of my greatest loss. Grief pressed on me harder with every conversation. I didn't know yet that I could stay with grief and not die from the pain. I still only knew how to leave.

I excused myself from the table, said my goodbyes, and looked for Dad. I found him engaged in a piecemeal sign language discussion with one of his deaf cousins. Dad had cut off the tip of his left thumb and most of his left and right index fingers in two separate jigsaw accidents, so he wasn't as deft at signing as he once was.

I waved at his cousin and indicated I was taking Dad away for a minute.

"I have to go," I told him.

He drew me in for a hug. "Thanks again, honey, for doing the eulogy. That was nice what you said about your grandma."

I pressed my face against his lapel. "I love you, Dad."

He patted my back. "I love you, too, Lynnie. Drive safe."

I walked out of the social hall, pulled my coat from the hanger on the coatrack, and slipped it on as I walked out the door. Cold air hit my face, air that smelled like the day I walked out the same door and got into a black car parked behind a hearse. I thought I'd gotten ahead of it, left those memories and grief in the social hall. I stood there, frozen, as the emptiness and nothingness weighed down my heart. In the distance, I heard a train whistle.

This is never going to end, is it?

Driving west on I-40 toward Little Rock, I catch up to a train heading in the same direction, its tracks parallel to the freeway, and I feel a familiar pinprick in my heart. Despite its heavy bags, grief travels readily.

Six weeks after surgery to repair a torn ligament when I was fourteen, the doctor removed the bandage. What remained was a thick, purple scar, which embarrassed me for years. I didn't value the scar for its protective qualities. Instead, I hid it however I could. I think about how grief has left a scar, too, an ugly reminder of what I've lost and how I hide from it however I can. I wonder if I'm ready to trust what Amy said—that grief is not supposed to end and that I can learn to live with it. Maybe not always in harmony, but without fear and avoidance.

In a few miles, the train disappears from the rearview mirror, and instead of mess with the radio and disengage, I stay with the question: am I ready?

CHAPTER 33

Larry and I arrive at his sister Carol's house. After we unload the car, we go see his mother.

When Lillian was diagnosed with Alzheimer's, she'd said to Larry, "This will be harder for you and the others than for me. Eventually, I won't know you, but you'll still know me."

She was right. Lillian hasn't known anyone for years, and the family grapples with the pain of watching her slow decline, not knowing when or how her life will end.

In the car, Carol warns us that Lillian no longer says much and that she spends most of her days in a chair or in bed sleeping or staring at nothing. Memories disappear as quickly as they're formed. Her disease has progressed to where she knows she likes cranberry juice only when she tastes it or loves daisies only when she sees them. She enjoys the sunshine but wouldn't understand if it was burning her skin.

We walk in the room, and she is sunk deep into the side of her recliner with her head on the armrest. Larry and Carol lift her upright, straighten her pillow, and cover her with a blue fleece. She sees me and holds out her hand.

"Who's this pretty lady?" she asks slowly. Her speech is somewhat garbled, but her accent is still unmistakable: Texas with a hint of New Orleans, where she was born and raised.

"Hi, Lillian," I say and take her hand. "I'm Lynn."

She smiles and nods her head, not in recognition but in polite acknowledgment.

I lay her hand back in her lap, and Larry sits down in the chair next to her.

"Hi, Mom," he says.

She looks over at him and her eyes brighten. She takes his hand and holds it to her cheek. While she doesn't speak his name, somewhere in her mind she seems to know he is her son.

Lillian remains quiet while the three of us talk to her and with each other. Larry picks up a framed photo from the dresser and shows it to her.

"Do you know who this is?" Larry asks, not expecting an answer.

"He never had a girl," she says, surprising all of us.

When Lillian was a child, her father died by suicide, and her mother's brother, fondly known as Uncle, moved in with the family and raised Lillian and her sisters as his own. The photo was of Uncle, and she was right. Uncle had a few girlfriends, but he remained single all his ninety-four years.

"That's right, Mom!" Larry says as Carol wipes away a tear.

Her words were like sunlight shining through murky water. A lucid, normal moment. A brief reprieve from the heaviness of the disease.

Lillian holds on to the photo as she falls asleep. Larry kisses her forehead.

"See you tomorrow, Mom," he whispers.

Later, as we get ready for bed, Larry says, "It was nice to connect with my mom again."

I know he's conflicted. He thought he'd made his peace with the fact that she'd never recognize him again, but today gave him hope, and he knows hope is futile with Alzheimer's.

"Let's pick up some flowers for her tomorrow," he adds. "She might not know they're there, but I will."

⊙ ⊙ ⊙

Shirley and David are stunned when they see me. Understandably, I suppose, but their praise makes me defensive.

It's the "You look wonderful" part that gets me, no matter who says it and with what intent, because what's implied, or at least what I hear, is that I didn't look wonderful before.

I was in eighth grade the first time someone called me "fat." My friend Robin had convinced me to try out for cheerleading, and I was in study hall when the results were read over the PA. Robin, Deb, another Deb, ". . . and Lynn Haraldson. Congratulations to our new junior-high cheerleaders."

I suspected nepotism. Robin's older sister was one of the judges. But I'd also had a pretty good tryout. Better than I expected. For a moment, I felt pretty good about myself. Then a boy sitting behind me said, "Great, we have a fat cheerleader!"

I turned around. He and three other boys were snickering. The study hall teacher called out, "Knock it off!" but the word was already out there.

I was a sensitive kid in general, and at fourteen, I'd also become self-conscious of my body, which had gone from scrawny to filled-out the minute I started my period the year before. I told Robin I was going to quit.

"They're idiots!" she said. "You're not fat. You can't quit."

Mom said I couldn't quit, either. "You're big-boned, Lynnie, not fat. Besides, boys only tease when they like you."

From then on, my weight seemed to became everyone's business. It didn't matter that I volunteered at a nursing home or had a strong work ethic or took good care of my parakeet. No one commented on those things, or if they did, what I heard was more an afterthought: "Lynnie, honey, are you sure you should eat that? Maybe those pants aren't what a girl like you should be wearing. I hear you saved a toddler from choking to death. That's nice. Have you heard if you eat half a grapefruit before dinner, you won't eat so much?"

I internalized that my body was bulky and in the way, an annoyance and embarrassment, and so I tried to hide it. I apologized for it and sucked it up when I heard, "You have such a pretty face . . ."

Only recently have I begun to examine how I speak about my body. Last year, at a doctor's appointment, when all I wanted was to weigh less than 200 pounds for the first time in six years, a woman I never saw changed my perspective.

A nurse called me back to the room with the scale. I took off my boots and coat and stripped down to a T-shirt and spandex shorts. My stomach was empty, and I'd hit the bathroom a few minutes earlier. I stepped on the scale and exhaled, like breath has weight. I didn't care if I weighed 199.9, so long as that first number wasn't a two.

I'm moving back to Onederland, I just know it!

When the screen stopped blinking, I saw two ones. Both in the wrong place: 201.1.

Damn it!

I grabbed my shoes and clothes and followed the nurse to the exam room across the hall.

I've worked so hard this time, changed so many things . . .

As I dressed, the nurse called another woman back to the room with the scale. Before she cleared my number, I heard the woman say, "Oh, I wish I weighed that."

I almost tripped over my pant leg.

What? Did she say she wants to weigh 200 pounds? Who wants to weigh 200 pounds?

You did, that's who. One hundred pounds ago. Remember?

I finished dressing and sat down. I thought about how weight has always been like a centipede crawling up my leg. *Get it off me, now! Give me normal cholesterol numbers now! Normal blood pressure now! No more prediabetes now!* I'd never offered kindness to the me who'd decided in the first place to normalize her health.

I silently thanked the woman who'd lamented her weight for helping me view bodies in a different light.

This new perspective was like when you buy a new car, and you notice the same make and model everywhere. A few months later, when I was helping Cassie plan her wedding, I made an appointment with a woman who had a wedding cake baking business in her home. She'd never met me and so, of course, had no idea I once weighed 300 pounds. At the time, I weighed about 170, and if it was the first time you had ever seen me, the thought might cross your mind that I was overweight. We sat down at her dining room table: the woman, me, and the woman's twenty-something daughter, whose leg was in a large metal brace.

We talked briefly about cupcakes when, out of nowhere, the woman outright apologized to me for her daughter's weight. The girl looked mortified but seemed used to her mother's behavior because she immediately launched into an explanation (read: she was apologizing, too). She was on some high school sports team when she was in a horrific accident that crushed her leg. Subsequently, she spent months in rehab and, apparently, gaining weight. Her mother then said, "She has such a pretty face, doesn't she? If only . . ." and in that moment, I thought I was going to lose my shit all over her unbelievably horrible parenting ass. Instead, I smiled at the girl and told her how sorry I was, and I didn't mean sorry for her weight.

A few weeks after Cassie's wedding, I was in our local coffee shop and the woman standing in front of me, who I knew vaguely, ordered a muffin and a mocha. When she turned and saw me, she said, "Oh, I know I shouldn't, especially standing next to you!"

I wanted to say that I understood, that I, too, had learned at some point in my life that fat people should apologize for making thinner people uncomfortable, apologize for their bodies, food choices, or even existing.

"I'm not the food police," I said. "What you choose to eat is no one's business."

But I suspect my words fell flat. *Easy for you to say* is what I would have been thinking if our roles were reversed. I had a lot to learn about communicating body positivity.

⊙ ⊙ ⊙

After spending Thanksgiving Day with my aunt and uncle, Larry and I return to his sister's house. I log onto the online weight loss community I joined a few years ago. Engaging with the community is the first time I've verbalized my struggle to accept my body. The people there understand the interconnectedness of weight and self-acceptance and how our thoughts about weight and grief are often integrated. What I appreciate most is their honesty. Maybe it's the quasi anonymity of being online, but not much gets sugarcoated unless we're actually discussing donuts or snickerdoodles.

"Why do people make such a big deal when someone loses weight?" I type into the chat. "I was just at my aunt and uncle's house, and they were all, 'You look great!' and I thought, I'm still the same person I was 150 pounds ago, right?"

"Have your aunt and uncle ever made your weight an issue?" someone writes.

"Not really," I write back.

"It sounds like you're the one making the big deal," writes someone else. "People are going to notice. Most of the time it has nothing to do with who you were before. And if you weren't good enough for them before, screw them, they're not worth your time!"

I need to understand what Shirley and David saw when I walked through their front door. I've taken photos of my face every month to note my weight loss, but I haven't compared them to photos at my heaviest. When we get home from Arkansas, I find the photo of Shirley and me sitting at my dining room table in 2004, and I scan it next to the one Larry took of us at her dining room table a few days ago. The comparison startles me, and not just because of the weight difference. I was still on Paxil in 2004. I wasn't smiling my usual toothy smile. I looked tired. I was tired. In the recent photo, I look confident. Happy. It is the face of someone who has learned a lot about herself.

I bring the photos to my next, and what will be my last, therapy session.

"I didn't notice it before, how visible those coping mechanisms were," I say to Amy. "I still cringe, though, when I look at my before body. I have a long way to go toward accepting myself. All the versions of myself."

We've discussed this before, the importance of acknowledging—without running away—all the things I am and have been and might be: someone who is sometimes depressed and sometimes not depressed, angry and not angry, anxious and not anxious, a sometime loner and a sometime attention-seeker, 300 pounds or 140 pounds. I carry all of me with me all the time, so I get to choose what kind of companion I want to be.

"Maybe you'll never get there, to full-body acceptance," Amy says. "But recognizing when and how you don't accept yourself allows you to respond with more self-compassion."

That makes sense, especially given what happened last weekend.

On Saturday, Larry and I had attended a party. A male acquaintance winked at me as he nudged Larry and asked, "What's it like to be with a completely different woman in bed?"

Amy's eyes fly wide open.

"I know! I was speechless!" I say.

"What did Larry say?"

"He said, 'She's the same beautiful woman I've always known.' So why don't I believe him?"

Larry had always told me I was beautiful, no matter what I weighed. But I never trusted any man to tell me the truth, especially if we were in bed. My truth was that my body was not beautiful, so, in my mind, that was every partner's truth, no matter what they said.

"I know Bruce loved my body because he loved me. And I know Larry loves my body because he loves me. I want to love my body because I love me, too."

Grief doesn't spring solely from an identifiable loss, Amy explains. We can grieve what we wish we had, too, and that includes love for and acceptance of ourselves. The grief I feel now, for the body I always wished I had, deserves to be acknowledged and honored, just like I'm learning to do with Bruce's death and other losses and trauma I've experienced.

"We've covered a lot of ground these last fifteen months," she says, closing her notebook. "Do you want another appointment?"

"I think I can leave the nest," I joke. But I am ready. At least for now. "Thank you for everything."

"You know where I am if you need me," she says, and we hug goodbye.

CHAPTER 34

I'm friends with a woman who is friends with a woman who, last month, met Courtney Love by chance in Hawaii, and they spent an evening in a hotel bar smoking cigarettes and talking. Courtney Love and I don't have much in common, but I'm sure we could throw back a few martinis discussing what we have in common: both of us were widowed soon after giving birth.

I read recently that she decided to sell Kurt Cobain's personal belongings: "My house is like a mausoleum. My daughter doesn't need to inherit a giant bag full of flannel shirts. A sweater, a guitar, and the lyrics to '(Smells Like) Teen Spirit'—that's what my daughter gets. And the rest of it we'll just . . . sell."

The dead leave behind a lot of ordinary stuff, from toothbrushes and books to cars with a bunch of crap stuffed under the seats. Stuff someone else has to deal with after they're gone. For twenty-four years, I've moved Bruce's things from apartment to apartment, storage to storage, house to house. Wherever I moved, he moved.

"I can't keep taking him with me everywhere I go. I think it's finally enough that he's right here," I said to the woman who knows the woman who met Courtney Love. I place my hand over my heart. "Time to hand over his stuff to Carlene and let her decide what to do with her father's things."

Time and therapy have softened the sting of going through Bruce's stuff. What used to be a razor cut through my heart when I'd touch the mask he wore when Carlene was born is now a soft sadness, no heavier than a toddler's feet padding across a bare floor. I'll always wish I didn't know this grief, but at least now, when it presents itself, I no longer send it to the corner like a punished child.

I page through our wedding album, remembering how nervous I was that day. Not because I was getting married but because I was getting married in front of a few hundred people.

"What if I faint?" I'd asked David.

"Don't lock your knees," he'd said. "And if you feel like you're going down, I keep smelling salts in my pocket."

In one of the photos, Bruce is sitting with his three groomsmen, one of whom is wearing white sweat socks. When I first saw the proof, I complained that the photo was ruined. Bruce said what he saw wasn't white socks but four handsome guys who couldn't wait to loosen their ties and have a beer.

Next up is his red International Harvester snapback cap. The foam lining has disintegrated to a fine powder, but the rest of the hat is in good condition. I shake it out and put it aside to wash. I'll hang it on a peg in my office with my other ball caps.

At the bottom of another box is the small blue travel log he kept when he participated in America's Youth in Concert the summer between his junior and senior years of high school. Shortly before we were married, I found the log in a box of his things he'd brought over from his parent's house. I shouldn't have, but I opened it and read to the third entry, which started with, "Shelly is a lot of fun."

Shelly, whoever she was, no longer intimidates me. I open the small volume and take in Bruce's handwriting, which I recognize as much as his face.

I didn't know he was in Philadelphia on the Fourth of July during the Bicentennial or that he performed at Carnegie Hall, Notre Dame ("Bad acoustics," he wrote), Montreux, St. Mark's Basilica in Venice, and St. Paul's in Rome.

He also went on a tour of Paris ("Boring!"), loved Geneva and

Innsbruck, danced in a disco in Florence, and lost his class ring in the Mediterranean Sea.

In the back of the journal are the names and addresses of two dozen other performers he met. The Toad the Wet Sprocket song "Walk on the Ocean" plays in my head as I wonder how long he stayed in touch with them. Did they send letters?

I close the journal and set it next to our wedding album. If I ever go to Europe, I will take it with me and write about the same places and things he saw, only I doubt very much that I'll find Paris boring. I might, though, throw my class ring in the Mediterranean.

The largest thing I've kept over the years is the Hitachi turn-dial thirteen-inch television my parents gave Bruce and me as a wedding gift. I won't give it to Carlene because what would she do with an ancient television? I decide to put it in the garage next to the pile of other things I am giving away.

A few days later, just before the men from the Salvation Army load it into their van, I cave and tell them to leave the TV.

I don't need a therapist to tell me why. Bruce touched it, he watched it, he moved the antennae around on it, and he rapped it a few times to get a better signal. We watched *Shogun*, *Winds of War*, *East of Eden*, *Family Ties*, *Fridays*, and *Saturday Night Live* on that TV. We hosted the 1983 Super Bowl party. Fourteen of our friends crowded around the screen. We fell asleep watching *The Tonight Show* the first few nights Carlene and I were home from the hospital. With no remote, we had to get up and change the channel, and I especially liked to watch Bruce walk to the TV and bend over to turn the knob. I can't give that memory away.

CHAPTER 35

The plane lands early on a Wednesday morning, and I wander, bleary-eyed, around the underbelly of the airport in search of the rental car counter. I reserved a practical car to get me around the state for the week, but Budget's idea of practical and mine are thankfully very different. A half hour later, I'm driving out of the parking garage in a cherry-red Dodge Caliber. I crank up the satellite radio, open the sunroof, and merge onto I-494 west. As my hair whips around in the wind, I breathe in the familiar air. Even blindfolded, I'd know it was July in Minnesota.

Cassie, her husband, and my ten-month-old granddaughter, Claire, will be on an early afternoon flight, and Carlene, driving out from Pennsylvania, will arrive later today. We're in Minnesota to visit my family and spend some time at my brother's vacation place on Lake Edward. Later in the week, I'll go to Jasper and Carlene will go to Luverne to see her grandma Eileen. She will join me in Jasper for the Haraldson family reunion and the all-class high school reunion.

Carlene inherited her father's nature. She takes seriously her role as Bruce's only child and is as devoted to his parents as he was. When Walt broke his hip in 2000, Carlene took a week off from school to be with him in the hospital, which she included in her senior project:

> I wanted to be there for him and take care of him. When I arrived, my grandmother was overjoyed. I could tell she needed me there with her. The sight of my grandfather was sad. He was so pale and frail. There wasn't any strength in

his body, and I could tell he was in a lot of pain. The only thing I could do was sit with him on his bed and hold his hand. I talked to him a little and helped him eat and drink. I gave him all the encouragement I could and gave him my love. I was with him every day and was with him before he went into surgery. He was a little scared, and I prayed he'd get through it fine. I knew my father was watching over him and perhaps, through me, offered his love as well.

Despite his pledge to make up for the way he treated me when Bruce was alive, keeping his mouth shut was *not* easy for Walt. When I didn't live up to his and Eileen's expectations, like getting pregnant and married within two years of Bruce's death, he got in his digs, especially about my weight. The first time he saw me after Cassie was born, he scolded me when I took a second helping of mashed potatoes.

"You've got quite a bit of weight on you," he said.

Keeping my years-old promise to Bruce, I'd said nothing, although I'd wondered what Bruce would have done if he had heard his father insult me again. Would he have defended me or remained silent? This is where Carlene and Bruce are different. Carlene is rarely afraid to speak her mind. If she'd been old enough to understand, I know she would have defended me, and most likely, he'd have listened because he worshipped her.

Walt passed away five years ago, a few weeks after Carlene graduated from high school. At the time, I was still reeling from her senior project and didn't feel up to a Bouwman family reunion, especially since I was well on my way to 300 pounds.

I hate that my insecurities prevented me from being with Carlene, even though she told me then and she still does now that it was fine with her that I didn't go. That's the nature part of her again. I didn't always go with Bruce to family functions, either. In the end, though, I realize that all of my not going, with Bruce or Carlene, was self-punishment, and like all regrets, I may never make complete peace with those decisions.

I check into my hotel and stop by my parents' townhouse to say a quick hello before heading to my appointment with David, who is now the pastor of a large church in a Minneapolis suburb. While there are other people I will see this week who are part of my grief story, David, aside from Bruce, is the most central and complicated part of that narrative.

Months after Carlene's project had concluded, I finally responded to his email, the one in which he'd apologized for preventing me from seeing Bruce's body. While I'd not yet done the deep dive into my grief, I knew enough that I could tell him I understood that he had suffered an unbelievable loss, too, and to assure him I knew his actions stemmed from his anguish over what was the right thing to do. It's only now that I realize how much of a presence he'd been in my early adult life, before and after Bruce died, and it's important that I let him know that his words and support during those years had a far-reaching impact on me.

I pull up to the church and take a moment to collect my thoughts. I wonder if he's feeling the same nervousness I am.

When I walk into the church, I can't see him, but I hear his deep, calming voice and follow it to an office down the hall. I find him standing in front of a desk talking to a secretary. He's gotten a bit gray, and I notice he still gestures with his hands when he talks.

"Hi, David," I say.

He turns around.

"Lynn!" He throws his arms in the air and buries me in a hug. "How are you? Come, let's talk in my office."

Just as he'd written in his email six years ago, the service folder from Bruce's funeral is pinned to the bulletin board behind him.

"I've thought about you so many times over the years. How is Carlene?" he asks, which starts a three-hour conversation in which we discuss Bruce's life and his death, my life afterward, David's life afterward, and what we've learned. He tells me about his work with native communities in South Dakota, and I share how meditation and Buddhist teachings have changed and grounded me. I tell him that I can finally talk about Bruce without feeling the profound sadness that kept me afraid for so many years, and I thank him for not leaving me when my grief was so new and raw.

As our conversation nears its end, I feel a healing take place deep inside and a burden lifted. When we say goodbye, another piece of my grief puzzle is set in place.

After another day in Minneapolis, it's time to head up to Lake Edward. I haven't seen a decent sunset since the last time I was in Minnesota. Sunsets in western Pennsylvania, while pretty, are brief. The sun disappears behind the hills and trees long before it actually sets. Here on the prairie, the sun sinks slowly, like butter soaking into a pancake. Driving between Big Lake and St. Cloud, I watch the long, lazy sunset and think about how the weather is one of the few things death doesn't change. I still sometimes check the forecast for Jasper on Bruce's birthday, Father's Day, and our anniversary, and I imagine the ways we'd celebrate the occasion based on the weather. If it's supposed to snow on his birthday, I would have gone to the grocery store early and made sure I had candles and coconut for a German chocolate cake. If it's sunny on Father's Day, Carlene and our other children—in my daydream, we always have more children—would give Bruce their homemade cards while we had a picnic in the field or down by the creek.

I don't check the forecast on the anniversary of his death, although I often daydream about that day with an alternate ending. Bruce stops at the tracks while the train passes. He comes in for our noon meal. He washes his hands in the sink at the foot of the stairs while I put the pork chops and mashed potatoes on the table. I nurse Carlene while we eat, and then hand her to my mom so I can get ready to go to Pipestone.

Bruce and I go to the grocery store, and as we walk down the baking aisle, he says, "I forgot to tell you that I made the banana cake mix on my birthday and brought it to play practice."

"That was nice of you," I'd say. "Was it any good?"

"Yes," he'd say. "Everyone liked it."

We pick out a bottle of champagne at the liquor store, maybe a bottle of blackberry brandy, too, then drive home listening to the radio. We sing and talk and don't think at all about trains or death. When we get home, I make coffee and warm up some muffins for afternoon lunch. Mom joins us, still holding Carlene, and I ask her if she put her down at all.

"No," she says and rubs her cheek over Carlene's peach-fuzz hair.

"Did the fuel guy come?" Bruce would ask, and mom says yes and that she gave him the check.

Afterward, Bruce starts chores and I start dinner. It's an ordinary day, not one I would remember the rest of my life.

◉ ◉ ◉

It's dark when I arrive at the lake. Claire is asleep. Everyone else is sitting on the deck in short sleeves and T-shirts, except Carlene, who is wrapped in sweatpants and a hoodie. Mosquitoes are always on that girl like flies on stink. I don't know if it's her neon-white skin like her father's or if they sense she has better tasting blood than the rest of us, but there isn't a mosquito in the state that doesn't know when Carlene is in town.

After a few hours of s'mores and laughter, we climb into our assigned beds or sleeping bags. In the morning, I'm awakened by a hummingbird at the screen window above where I'm sleeping. Claire is rummaging through my suitcase. My parents are talking on the deck. Matthew is making eggs and bacon. He'll soon get the boat ready for a morning of fishing with Dad and my son-in-law. There isn't a cloud in the sky. The lake is sparkling. Soon I will be back on the road, on my way to Jasper.

The drive there takes me around the outskirts of the southern Minneapolis suburbs, which have expanded exponentially. Once out of the sprawl, not much has changed. In LeSuer, the Jolly Green Giant still greets passersby from his cutout billboard, the speed limit through St. Peter (where, in earlier days, I accumulated five speeding tickets) is still thirty-five mph, and Big Boy—balancing a plate of hamburgers—stands large in the restaurant parking lot in Mankato.

I get on Highway 30 just outside Madelia, which will take me to Pipestone. A half hour later, I've passed two tractors and no cars. I look down at the speedometer. Seventy-five miles an hour. Happens every time I'm on these flat, straight country roads. I back off the gas a little.

In Pipestone, I take a left at the municipal pool where I spent many summer afternoons with my friends. Several miles later, I decide to take a detour and drive past the house Bruce and I rented after we were married. There are no vehicles in the driveway, so I pull in and park.

The place hasn't changed much in twenty-five years. A fresh coat of paint is all. The garage door is still missing.

The tree in the backyard sparks a memory I haven't thought about since I lived here. Before we adopted Miss Kitty and Festus, someone gave us a kitten they'd found. She couldn't have been more than six weeks old. I forget what we named the tiny black-and-white ball of fuzz, but she was a real spitfire who insisted on sleeping between us. We'd only had her a week when Bruce and I came home from a wedding and found her on the living room floor lying in her feces, crying. She couldn't walk.

Distemper, most likely. Bruce had seen it before in barn cats.

Gingerly, I picked her up and placed her on a towel. I rubbed her lightly behind her ears as Bruce and I talked about what to do. We agreed she was too young, too tiny to survive until Monday when we might get a vet appointment. She had to be put down, and we knew without saying that it wouldn't be me who did it.

We didn't have a rifle, so we walked over to the neighbors across the road and asked to borrow one of theirs. I stayed with them while Bruce did the deed, and even though I put my fingers in my ears, I heard the gunshot. He came to get me after he'd buried her under the tree behind the house.

Walking home, I asked if he was okay. He said it was never easy to do the right thing. I didn't press him for more. After the miscarriage, I began to understand that, although Bruce didn't express his feelings as readily as I did, he was as emotionally complex as me.

I often wonder who we'd be today if we'd had the chance to mature together. It's a question I can't answer, of course, but if what we'd started while living here had been allowed to grow, we would know each other in a way I can never know anyone else now.

There are things that therapy can't fix; it can only examine. One of them is the lingering effects of traumatic loss as a young adult. Bruce's death conditioned me to fear the same thing happening again, and while I can now acknowledge and understand that fear, I can't unknow it. The wall I built to protect myself isn't as high anymore, but it's still there and always will be.

This house represents unfettered intimacy, and rather than grieve that I will never know that kind of closeness again, I am grateful to have known it at all.

A few miles later, I arrive at my cousin Dean's farm, where I'm staying for the weekend. I park next to a car in front of his house. Two older women get out. Thinking they are extended family in town for the reunion, I introduce myself.

"Hi, I'm Lynn, Don's daughter."

One of the women reluctantly shakes my hand as she looks with concern at the other woman.

"I'm looking for Dean," she says.

"Oh. I'm sorry. He's in Pipestone. He'll be home in an hour."

"Well, we're burying my brother tomorrow, and I need to drop him off."

Oh.

"He's in the trunk."

OH!

Dean mentioned that he mowed the cemetery across the road, but I had no idea he was the gravedigger, too.

She opens the trunk, and the two women lift out a medium-sized cardboard box.

"Well . . . um . . . I guess you should . . ." I look around, wondering what to do. "How about you bring him in the house?"

I hold open the back door, and when the women are inside, I look desperately around the kitchen.

"You can put him over there," I say, pointing to a space on the floor next to the microwave cabinet.

They set down the box, offer a terse thank-you, and walk out the door.

I stand there for a moment looking at the box before I call Dean. I get his voicemail.

"I have no idea who this guy is, but he's on your kitchen floor," I say at the beep.

⊙ ⊙ ⊙

I thought about Sam during the four-hour drive to Jasper and debated whether to deliberately see him today or risk running into him later. Either way, it was going to happen. It's impossible to avoid anyone in a town this small. If he was still angry at me for what happened the last time I saw him, I wanted him to tell me in person rather than see the indifference on his face in the crowded bar or at the street dance.

I text Dean that I'm going to town and will be back later. On my way, I stop at Lisa and Curt's. Pulling into their driveway, I see that their two-story white house is still encircled by an elm and a linden tree on the east side and a maple in the back. In the front, an apple, ash, and birch reach up a story and a half, keeping the house cool, as cool as it can be in the summer on the prairie. I park on the side of the house near the garage. Their dog, Lucy, barks and circles my car. She doesn't remember me, but I'm not afraid. She's a lab mix. The worst she'll do is try to lick me to death.

"Hey, good girl!" I lean over and pet her ears. "Where's your mama?"

She bolts toward the barn. I'm almost certain that's not where Lisa is, so I walk up to the back porch. Six cats are perched on the railing. Black-eyed Susans in full bloom line the back side. Beans, peas, and pumpkins overflow the chicken wire surrounding the garden.

The smell of something tomatoey cooking on the stove hits my nose just before I open the screen door.

"Lisa?" I call out.

"In the kitchen!" I hear her tap a spoon on the side of a pot.

Just inside, to my right, is the laundry room, which leads to a bathroom. I peek in and see that there's still no curtain on the window directly in front of the toilet.

"What if someone's out there?" I'd said the first time I was in their house.

"If someone's watching you pee from the middle of the trees, we have a problem," Lisa said.

I walk into the kitchen. "Hello!"

"Lynn! Oh, my gosh!" She sets down the spoon, and we hug. "Come in! How are you?"

"I can't stay long. I just wanted to pop in and say hi and let you know I made it."

She clears off a stool at the island in the middle of the kitchen. "Sit! I'm just making some sauce. Can I get you anything? Pop? Coffee?"

"No, I'm fine," I say, looking around. "The place looks great!"

"Oh, you know . . ." she says apologetically. "I can never keep up with it!"

Every inch of the refrigerator is filled with photographs. Among the smiling babies and children is the most recent Christmas photocard of my daughters, their husbands, my stepsons, and my granddaughter. My life has gone on, but it is here on their farm that I'm reminded of what could have been, where I witness how my life might have unfolded within a beautifully chaotic and sometimes difficult farm life and, hopefully, unshakeable marriage. I can't know what our future would have held, whether we would have survived the farm crisis or if Bruce would have grown his hair and joined a band, but before he died, our projected life was on the farm and together, so it's the only one I imagine with any certainty.

Curt walks in the back door and sees me sitting at the island.

"Hey!" he says. "I didn't know whose car that was out there."

"It's fancy, just like me." I stand up and give him a hug. "It's good to see you."

Curt's about the same height as Bruce was, around six feet, and his shirt smells of hay and cows.

The first time Bruce, Curt, and I were together was at a party a few days after the Styx concert. Throughout the evening, we were each pulled into other conversations, but when the party broke up, the three of us went to Curt's. I made us breakfast, and we talked until 4 a.m. Afterward, I drove Bruce back to his car in town. He said there was another party the following weekend and asked if I wanted to go.

I couldn't speak. I only nodded.

"Great! I'll pick you up around seven." He leaned over and kissed me lightly, no tongue, no other body parts. Just a soft, warm kiss.

I release Curt from our hug and swallow a lump in my throat. It's like ripping off a bandage every time I see him.

"How long are you in town?" he asks.

"I'll head home on Monday." I straighten my shirt and wipe a finger under my wet eyes. "Right now, though, I need to go."

"Come back for dinner!" Lisa says.

"I will." I hug her again and walk out the back door and across the porch, past the cats, past the tomatoes and cantaloupes, and past Lucy, who gets up and follows me to the car.

In town, I drive past the high school, the Lutheran church, and the town hall. There aren't many businesses still open downtown other than the bar, the bank, and Sam's shop. The former Haraldson's Grocery sits empty.

A knot forms in my stomach. Not the happy butterfly kind I used to feel before I saw Sam. This one feels like I've swallowed a chain-link fence.

The bay door is open. I park on the street and get out of the car.

Okay, Lynn, remember, you're doing this because you care about him and your friendship. You're doing this because you want to say you're sorry. You're doing this because you need to know he doesn't hate you.

But what if he doesn't want to talk to you?

Oh, come on, Lynn, knock it off! You're not twenty-four anymore. This isn't the Holiday Inn in Mankato. This is you being mature and understanding. You can handle anything that happens.

I walk in the shop and look around. "Sam?"

"Just a minute!" he calls out from the back.

Everything's the same as the last time I was here, when my heart was hopeful but bound in Bubble Wrap.

Sam walks in. He sees me and smiles.

That's good, right?

"Hey!" he says.

I walk over and hug him. "How are you?"

He hugs me back. "It's good to see you. Come on in."

I follow him to his office.

"Wow, how long has it been?" he asks.

Our conversations always begin with time. It's how we measure our relationship, in years apart. We never committed to the time it would take to wade through our wonder of each other or mediate the doubt that we could have a real relationship. We had hours. Hours of sex and talking. But hours don't create years when one or both of you is afraid.

I catch him up on my life and he catches me up on his. He has all the things he's ever wanted: a solid marriage, kids, a home, and good neighbors. He seems genuinely happy and confident about the decisions he made to make his life what it is, and the more we talk, it's clear that within that life is a place for a resuscitated friendship, a relationship free of chaff and craving.

Talking to Sam is like spreading jam on warm bread. His

familiar voice, like David's, is comforting. It eases me into my past here in Jasper, at least the simpler parts. I'm aware of the losses I suffered here. They revolve around me like a satellite. But sometimes, like now, they are out of range.

Sam looks at the clock. "Ah, man, I got some things to finish up before five."

I look at the clock, too. *How did two hours go by? I'm not ready to say goodbye!*

"Do you want to get a drink after I close up?"

I smile, happy he feels the same way. "Yes, but here? In town? People will wonder who that blond is you're with."

"Let 'em talk!" he says.

I have an hour.

Dean is home from Pipestone when I get back to his farm.

"I'm having dinner at Lisa's," I say, dropping my car keys on the table and taking off my shoes.

"So am I," he says.

"Great! See you there!"

I run up the stairs and take a shower. After drying my hair, I put on jeans and a cotton blouse that drapes too low over my cleavage. I swap it out for another shirt. Too clingy.

I'm not dressing for Sam. I'm dressing for the bar. The last time I was there was the day of Bruce's funeral. People talked then. They'll talk now. I don't want to offer them any fuel.

I settle on a loose scoop-neck T-shirt before running back down the stairs and out the door. I crank the air-conditioning in the Caliber to dry off the sweat. Five minutes later, I park in front of the bar and reapply my lipstick.

Deep breath. *You've got this!*

I walk in prepared to adjust my eyes to dim light, and for a moment, I'm confused. The place is no longer dark and mysterious like a Hitchcock film, and the back door isn't propped open to let out the smoke. It's well-lit and doesn't smell like rancid liquor and musty vinyl.

People at the bar turn to see who walked in. They don't recognize me, and I'm sure they'll ask each other, "Who is that?"

Whatever . . .

Sam is sitting at a table opposite the bar. I sling my purse over a chair across from him. "I hardly recognize the place!"

He starts to stand. "What do you want to drink?"

"Sit. I'll get something."

I walk up to the bar. I see the glances in my periphery. *There's no use trying to look nonchalant, people. Ask, I'll tell you who I am. Just don't make up shit about Sam.*

"What can I gettcha?" I don't recognize the bartender, but it doesn't mean I don't know him. We all change in twenty-four years.

"Do you have any wine?" He pulls a gallon bottle of dark red from the cooler. I crinkle my nose. He laughs and puts it back. I order a beer instead.

"Bud Light?" he asks.

When in Rome . . .

"Sure," I say.

I grab my beer and sit down. "This place has really changed. I won't need two showers to get the smell out!"

We pick up our conversation where we left off at the shop, sticking to a script of generalities and non-intimate memories. His phone rings. I don't ask. This isn't a Bon Jovi song.

"I'll be right back," he says.

I look around the bar and take in the changes and the people who've gone back to their conversations and pool game. *What is it about this town that draws me here? Friends, certainly. Family history, yes. Bruce isn't here, but he's always here. And then there's that question about the train. That's not it, though. Or at least not all of it. Not this time.*

Sam returns to his seat. "Sorry 'bout that."

"Not a problem. I've just been wondering why I keep coming back here."

He laughs. "To this bar?"

I roll my eyes. "You know what I mean. Why do I feel safe here? And I don't mean safe like physically safe. I mean emotionally safe, which I don't get because here is where the worst thing in my life happened."

I sip my beer and wait for Sam's profound answer.

"That was hard for all of us," he says. "We all miss him."

"I know, I know. But you'd think I'd never want to see any of you again, let alone this town."

We look at each other and say nothing. We both know the answer is bigger than anything we could talk about in this bar in the course of an hour.

I look away. I have to let him go home. "Well . . ."

Sam nods.

"It was really fun to catch up, but I've gotta go," I say.

He throws back the rest of his beer. "Yep, me, too."

Outside, we start our goodbye. We both know it will be years, if ever, before we are together like this again.

"Oh, wait!" I get my phone from my purse. "We have no pictures of us! Let's take a selfie."

We put our heads together, and I raise my phone at arm's length and snap the photo. We look at it and laugh. No model pose, nothing fake, just our smiling faces and our history etched in the creases around our eyes.

Sam pulls me in for a hug. "It was good to see you again. You'll be in town tomorrow, right?"

"Yep," I say and kiss his cheek. "See you then."

I get in my car and watch him walk down the street. I check in with my feelings by sitting with my breath for a few minutes. Do I have any regrets? Not really. I wasn't ready to be a partner to Sam or to anyone years ago, as demonstrated by my failed relationships after him. If anything, I probably spared us both a lot of heartache by changing my mind that night in the hotel, even though my decision came from an emotionally unhealthy place.

Now I feel a deep sense of contentment with our friendship and contentment that another piece of the grief puzzle is set in place.

CHAPTER 36

Driving into town the next day, I notice the front doors of the high school are open. When the Jasper school district merged with Pipestone's more than ten years ago, someone with big dreams and little capital bought the building for five dollars with plans to turn it into an apartment complex. Instead, it's just another old building in a small town, ignored and in disrepair.

The Jasper High School mascot—called a "Quartzsiter—was a cartoon caveman carrying a club in one hand and shading his eyes with the other while looking off in the distance. A building downtown houses Quartzsiter memorabilia and the framed photographs of every graduating class since 1912 that used to hang in the halls. When I went to school here, I always felt like part of a legacy when I walked past those pictures, many of which included family members.

I haven't been inside the school in more than twenty years, and since Carlene won't be in town for another hour, I park on the street and walk up to the building. Feeling a little like an intruder, but also like a Quartzsiter, I walk through the front doors.

The hallway is dark. No one is here, at least in this part of the building. The air is cool and smells old. Not old like my former antique store but unattended old. Musty and dank. I walk down the hall to an open side door that leads to the stage of the auditorium. I peer inside and a chill runs through me, like I'm in the presence of a thousand ghosts. Lit only by the sunlight coming through the ten-foot glass block windows and a door propped open in the back, the entire space looks like a sepia photograph, stuck in time. No dust dances in the streaks of sunlight, no energy pulses through its walls. But like a friend you haven't seen in years, whose hair is now gray and skin is now wrinkled and worn, their eyes are the same piercing color you remember, their smile still as bright, and you recognize them immediately.

I walk out onto the stage about twenty feet. The house curtains have been removed, making it possible from where I stand to have a full view of the few hundred seats on the main floor and balcony.

I've been on this stage many times for gym class, band and choir concerts, and, of course, cheerleading, which I didn't quit. I think of the boy and his friends who called me fat, a few of whom I'll probably see later today. I doubt they remember that they laughed at me all those years ago, but if I do see them, I won't ask them why they did what they did or tell them I've forgiven them. I also won't tell them that I'll never forget how they made me feel.

Where I'm standing is almost the exact spot where I put on the Snoopy costume our choir director, Bob Jones, convinced me to wear on stage during the performance of "You're a Good Man, Charlie Brown." After our choir sang, I had only a minute to take off the costume while he introduced the next song, "Fifty Nifty United States." As I walked back on stage to take my place on the second riser, the audience started laughing. Mr. Jones looked up at me, smiled, and tapped his finger just below his nose. The pipe cleaner whiskers were still on my face. I could have died! I peeled them off and balled them up in my hand, but it was a few more seconds before everyone stopped laughing.

Oh, how I hate being the center of attention! Unlike Bruce, whose spirit permeates this stage. He was a natural performer, spontaneous, comfortable, and confident in front of an audience.

I walk out a little further, remembering the homecoming coronations, graduations, and plays I'd witnessed from the audience. On the day before Christmas break, students in all grades packed into the auditorium to watch a movie. When I was in seventh grade, they showed *The Pit and the Pendulum*;

in eighth, the *House of Usher*; and in ninth, *Wait Until Dark*.

I take a few pictures before walking back to the hallway. I look to my right past the art room and the girls' locker room and down Quartzsiter Hall where we practiced tornado drills. If I weren't alone, I might wander around, find my locker, and walk through the old study hall, but the ghostly cold still rubs my skin, and I decide I've seen enough.

⊙ ⊙ ⊙

When Bruce took Carlene and me home from the hospital, I'd sat in the middle of the back seat next to her car seat. The usual forty-minute trip took over an hour since Bruce drove like the baby was perched on top of the car. After he pulled into our garage, Bruce hopped out and came around to retrieve his daughter. He wanted to carry her across the threshold, he said, which was fine with me since walking (with all that was going on down below) was a delicate thing.

Our dog trotted into the garage just as Bruce was settling Carlene into the crook of his arm.

"Hey, Duke! This is Carlene!" he said, tilting his arm. Duke growled. Bruce held Carlene a little tighter. "Well, you're gonna have to get used to her."

Today will be the first time Carlene and I have been in Jasper, just the two of us, since her baptism. I don't know why I'm so nervous about it. Both Carlene and Cassie have been here with me before. But they only ever saw my grandmothers, aunt Mavis, and Lisa and Curt on those trips. I always kept the broader Jasper me private, mostly because that person felt too hard to explain. Now, I wonder if I'm trying to prove to my daughter my relevance in Jasper by showing her off or if I'm still trying to prove it to myself.

I meet Carlene in front of the bowling alley. When she was

eight years old and Cassie was six, we took both my grandmothers out to lunch here. Whatever the reason for Katinka's and Signe's tepid relationship, I loved both of them, and I also wasn't taking them to lunch separately. They had to live with each other for an hour at the bowling alley, and they did.

"This was a great place to hang out back in the day," I say, peering in the window.

We walk up the street to the building that used to be my dad's store. Along the way, I tell her a few stories about what it was like to live here as a kid.

"Jasper isn't perfect, God knows, but I liked that I could go anywhere and people knew me. Made me feel special, I guess."

I ask someone walking by to take a photo of us in front of the store before we join a few former classmates on the other side of the street. The parade will start soon. We'll ride on the back of a flatbed that Dean will haul with his truck. My friend Jeanine makes the sign for the class of '81, and a couple guys load two cases of Bud Light on the back. Thank God I brought along a travel mug of Pinot.

We line up on the parade route near the old grade school. The Jasper Blowhards brass band is in a wagon in front of us, and I see Bruce's brother Doug on a flatbed with his graduating class. If I run into him later, I'll say hi, but I won't make an effort to find him. Doug looks and sounds just enough like Bruce to break my heart a little every time I see him, and God knows there are enough reminders of Bruce around me today.

As we proceed down the parade route, Carlene and I call out to my parents, who are sitting on the lawn of the high school with their former classmates. I haven't spent any time alone with Mom during this trip, a conscious choice that was met with bitter accusations wrapped in guilt-riddled language. But as hard as her words have been to hear, I'm better at letting them fall away instead of sink in. I'm glad to see Mom sitting next to her friends, talking and laughing. I will always want her to be happy, but I will no longer facilitate it at my expense.

When the parade is over, Carlene and I walk around downtown, which is packed with people, more than actually live here. We run into Sam, who tells us that Carlene, the woman who inspired Carlene's name, is there somewhere. After a few minutes, I spot a woman with shoulder-length brown hair talking to Robin's sister, the one who probably made me a cheerleader.

I tap her on the shoulder. "Carlene?"

The woman turns around. "Lynn!"

I'm relieved that she recognizes me.

When Carlene sees Carlene, she gasps. "I'd know you anywhere," she says, and I feel like a circle has closed now that the two Carlenes have finally met.

As the sun sets, the band warms up for the street dance. I imagine that Bruce and I would stay for the first part of the dance and then join his friends at his thirtieth class reunion. Curt told me about it and Lisa offered to take me, but I haven't seen most of those folks since Bruce died, and I feel like I've paraded Carlene around enough for one day. We stay for another hour before heading back to Dean's.

Carlene quickly falls asleep, but I'm wired and a little drunk, so I sit on the floor at the end of the bed and look out the window at the lightning flashing from a thunderhead about twenty miles southwest—too far away to hear thunder. With little in the way of acoustics, sound dissipates quickly on the prairie. Not like in Pennsylvania, where thunder bounces off the mountains and trees and scares the bejesus out of my dogs (and sometimes me).

That's not to say things don't get loud out in Minnesota during a storm. If you're right under it, you'll hear it.

I was terribly afraid of storms when I was a kid. Sometimes, I'd run into my parents' room and Dad would offer me his arm to lay on. Sometimes, I'd sit in my closet with the door shut and read by flashlight. As I watch the storm slowly move southeast, I think about how Bruce's death was unlike any storm I'd ever been through. It scared me, and I reacted to that fear by running away. Now I know that I can be scared and stay. I don't have to like grief, but it's less painful when I don't run away.

I crawl into bed and fall asleep imagining, one more time, what Bruce and I might be doing right now.

At the slightest hint of sunlight, I wake up. Carlene is lying on her side facing the wall and still holding her blankie, the one she's had since she was born. When I bought it at the JC Penney in Pipestone, it was bright yellow and fluffy and had a satin edge. Now it's a dull, almost white color, flat, frayed, and missing the edge—which Carlene called "the soft"—despite the number of times her grandma Eileen sewed it back on.

Carlene once gave her blanket to a high school boyfriend like it was a letter jacket. When I found out, I demanded she get it back immediately.

"It's mine!" she'd argued. "I can do anything I want with it! You just don't like him."

It was true. I didn't like her boyfriend. Not one bit. But her blanket held history—hers, mine, and her father's—and I knew there would be no history with the boyfriend, despite her insistence that she "loved" him.

I watch Carlene for a few minutes. I've always envied how she can sleep through almost anything, just like Bruce. Although he was a farmer, he wasn't a fan of early mornings. I can still hear Walt rapping on the door at the foot of the stairs to wake him up. Three sharp knocks, then "Bruce! Chores!"

While Bruce never complained to his father about what he thought were early mornings, he complained about them to me once in a while. In one of his letters, he told me how he had to help his brother load pigs "bright and early" at 7 a.m. one morning:

"That's bad enough," he wrote. "Only one thing would be worse and that's if you were in bed with me and I had to leave. That will be so nice when we are married. Sleeping with you will be great! I can hold you, or we can talk, or we can make love! We might even sleep part of the night!"

I get up and take a shower before waking Carlene. We're attending the community church service at my former church this morning. I ran into Bob Jones yesterday and he said he would be directing the choir, and we both agreed that Bruce would have certainly participated.

Mom and Dad are waiting for us in the narthex of the church.

"Did you bring any Lifesavers?" I ask Dad. He'd usually have Lifesavers in his suit pocket to keep us kids occupied during the sermon.

"Nope, but I have Rolaids!"

If Dad had forgotten the Lifesavers, he'd offer us Rolaids. "Seriously?"

He laughs. "I'm just kidding!"

"Did you have fun yesterday?" Mom asks Carlene.

"I did!" Carlene says. "Got to see a side of Mom I didn't know about!"

I can't deny I'd gotten a little rowdy during the parade because Carlene has the pictures to prove it.

"Let's just . . . not go there," I say and wave us into the sanctuary.

Except for the carpeting, things are the same as the last time I was here. The pews creak when we sit down, and Jesus is still knocking on a door in the center of the stained glass windows. The room is filled with voices as people turn around in their seats to greet their neighbors and friends.

After the service, Carlene and I find Bob Jones gathering sheet music on the organ.

"Hi, Bob."

He turns around. "Hello, again!"

When he sees Carlene, he draws a sharp breath.

"Carlene, this is Bob."

She holds out her hand. "It's nice to meet you finally."

Bob's eyes tear up as he takes her hand. "Oh, my dear, I'm so happy to meet you, too. Your father . . . he was such a wonderful man."

Carlene smiles. She's heard that many times this weekend.

"It's all so . . ." I start to say.

Bob understands what I can't articulate.

"We all miss him very much," he says.

In his sermon at our wedding, David referred to this church as holy space.

"Not because of the altar and symbols or the vestments I am wearing," he'd said. "It is holy because this is where we can be here for one another and, together, find a powerful peace."

As painful as my grief can be, as large a void as Bruce has left in my life, being here with Bob and Carlene in this space, I'm at peace. Not a big "Everything's gonna be great!" peace but a tender peace that resides alongside the grief and void.

Something else David had said at our wedding that meant a lot to Bruce was "Live fully for each other and live fully with each person you meet as you walk through your lives." I don't normally presume to know what Bruce would have wanted or done had he lived, but I know in all certainty that he would be glad that Bob, Carlene, and I were together here, missing him and, at the same time, remembering his kind and gentle spirit.

CHAPTER 37

I wake up on Monday to weather that is appropriately dismal for what I have planned to do before leaving Jasper. Carlene went back to Eileen's yesterday, and I'll be in Minneapolis later today for my flight back to Pennsylvania, but first, there are a few places I need to see.

After I pack up the car and say goodbye to my cousin, I go to the cemetery across the road. Grandma Katinka's brother Robert, who died when he was six weeks old, is buried there next to his mother, my great-grandmother Alexandra. No one ever talked about Robert or other children who died at young ages other than to say, "That's just the way things were back then."

I recently read a family history written by another of Katinka's brothers, and he included a few details surrounding Robert's death. Erling wrote how, around 8 a.m. on February 8, 1917, Robert screamed out from a pain that seemed to originate in his belly. Alexandra held him as she made oatmeal for the other children before they walked to school, but Robert could not be comforted. After two hours, he was still in distress, and Alexandra and her husband, Mathias, decided to baptize him. Mathias hailed two neighbors who were driving their sleigh past their farm and asked them to be Robert's godparents.

A few minutes after he was baptized, Robert died. They laid him out in the parlor, the coldest room in the house, and Mathias went to Jasper to purchase a casket. Using pickaxes and crowbars, neighbors dug a grave through six feet of frozen ground. Erling wrote how, on the day of the funeral, "There was much unabashed crying. The crying, I remember, was accompanied by audible sobbing. The congregation acted out the injunction, 'Weep with those who weep.'"

Standing at Robert's grave, I imagine the sobbing that took place in this spot ninety years ago—a completely appropriate response to grief, yet no one else in my family ever mentioned it.

I look over at Alexandra's grave. I can't begin to know the anguish she and Mathias felt as their baby cried and how they'd feared enough for his life to baptize him.

I walk down the next aisle to the grave of my great-grandfather Syver's first wife, who died the day after giving birth to her only baby. She was nineteen years old. It would be ten more years before Syver married my great-grandmother Mathilda, whose death gave me my first taste of grief.

I leave the cemetery and drive to Jasper. At the edge of town is the former grade school, now an assisted-living facility, and I pull into a parking space that faces Signe's former house.

When her husband, my grandfather Martin, died, Signe was so distraught that she never wanted to hear Martin's name spoken again. My dad, named after his father, was called by his middle name after that.

On the outside, it would seem that Signe had become something of a maverick after Martin died. She went back to teaching country school and obtained a loan to buy the house, which she fixed up as a boardinghouse for single female schoolteachers. For extra money, she made donuts on Saturdays and sent my dad down the street selling them for "two bits a dozen." Dad never got more than three blocks from home before running out.

I respect Signe and all she did to survive and raise her children, but I am sad that she shared none of her grief with me. When Bruce died, she was the only person I knew who understood what I felt, and yet, harnessed to a similar yoke as me, she never talked about Martin or his death, even when I pressed her. Signe only let me know her as a fun grandma who brought books, crayons, and puzzles when she visited, played Candyland and Canasta whenever I asked, and let me add too many drops of pink food coloring to the frosting when she made Aunt Sally cookies. She always had a pack of Beech-Nut in her purse, kept a bottle of Southern Comfort in the refrigerator, and never missed *The Lawrence Welk Show*. I really wish I could have known the other woman, too—the grieving widow—but Signe kept those feelings buried deep.

In his book, Erling also mentions—and that's all it is, a five-line mention—that in 1930, his sister Alpha was driving home to Minnesota from Illinois with the man she was to marry and, somewhere in Iowa, their car was struck by a train. Alpha was not hurt, but her fiancé died. I knew Alpha. I talked to her several times after Bruce died, and she never mentioned it. No one did.

At Robert's funeral, tender hearts cried, and I'm sure Alexandra's tender heart never fully recovered. Alpha's tender heart and Signe's tender heart probably never fully recovered, either. I know mine hasn't. No one's grief ends when the last dirt is thrown on the grave.

My family's avoidance and stoicism were nothing more than masked fear, and I'm glad I'm finally tired of being afraid. Talking about my grief has relieved my heart of some of its burden, and it breaks for those who lived before me who bore their pain in silence.

Enough mist has gathered on the windshield to blur the view of the house, and I don't know if it's God or Bruce or the ghost of my grandma, but the song "Dust in the Wind" starts to play on the radio.

I am thirty feet from my former sixth-grade classroom, one-hundred yards from the football field, a mile from his grave.

Yeah, Universe, I get the message. Nothing lasts forever.

I start the car and move on to my final destination.

⊙ ⊙ ⊙

Eileen used to take Carlene to Jasper to put flowers on Bruce's grave, and she always insisted on photographing her kneeling next to his headstone. Carlene hated it, said it felt creepy, but she never told her grandma.

Nothing ever happens at his grave, though, and it's why I'm not going there today. Not that I expect some grand revelation delivered by an aberration that rises up from the ground, but I've always thought that some small gesture of acknowledgment that I was there would be nice.

A friend whose husband died told me that she believes he reaches out to her through the wind chimes on her porch. Practical me says no, it's just the wind, but grieving me is on board. Is it so bad to hang on to something that helps us over the worst of the pain, something to believe in while we sort it all out? I don't think so, but Bruce only comes around in my dreams, and I know it's not really him because he would never intentionally hurt me. Still, I wonder if that's all I get. No wind chimes, just random, lousy dreams.

I drive the length of downtown Jasper one last time, past the high school, our old grocery store, and Sam's, and take a left on Highway 23. I continue for two and half miles south, then a half mile west, before I park fifteen feet from the tracks and get out of the car.

While I'd spent a good number of years living on the prairie, its fields of rocks and grass still intimidate me. The sky is more expansive than the land, reminding me how small and insignificant I am, especially standing here on this particular dirt road.

Cows moo in the distance, a few birds chirp. The fog has lifted, but it's still cool and cloudy. I've been here a few times before, and the same thing that happens at his gravesite happens at his place of death. Nothing. I'm not even sure why I'm here other than it seems like the appropriate final place to visit on the Grief Tour.

No one would know that someone died here. It's just a ditch like any ditch anywhere. Grass on one side, corn on the other. There's a stop sign now at the crossing, which seems moot. I look to the southwest at what used to be our farm. No Bouwmans live there anymore.

From a half mile away, it looks the same. Two silos—one working, one not. The barn is still there, although it could stand some repair. A corner of the second story of the house is visible, the side where Bruce's bedroom used to be. At night on those weekend visits so many years ago, Bruce and I would lie for hours in his bed, the light from the stereo receiver glowing orange. We'd talk, listen to music, and, when his parents weren't home, make love.

I hear a faint train whistle to the north and wonder if I should stay and watch it pass.

Six weeks after Bruce died, I'd had a dream. We were sitting on the couch in our living room, and I asked him how he could be killed by a train while crossing tracks he'd known were there all his life. Bruce answered calmly, "I didn't hear it."

I didn't understand. "How do you not hear a train?"

He smiled and said, "I love you. I have to go now."

I feel a tired old anger rise up. *I'm standing right here, Bruce. I can hear a train miles away. How did you not hear the one that was right next to you?*

I hear the whistle again and decide to stay. I take a few photos, walk back to the car, and sit down in the driver's seat, leaving the door open. I think about the letter Rodney wrote me when his daughter was born:

I remember those heady days, when it seems like you have the world by the tail: a loving wife, a job you love, the home you've always dreamed of and wanted, and especially when a new little baby daughter has entered your life. Well, I remember I felt invincible, like I would live forever and nothing bad could ever touch me.

I can, I think, get a notion of what was in Bruce's mind and heart that day. On the tractor, which is always a good feeling, all that horsepower at your fingertips. The open air of the countryside, even in the tractor cab. Beautiful young wife at home preparing a meal, your new daughter ready to be held in your hands. I believe when that sudden and tragic end came, Bruce was one of the happiest men on earth.

A minute more passes. I glance to the left and watch birds fly out of the cornfield. A second later, I glance to my right, and in the time it takes to blink, a twenty-four-year-old question is answered.

I jump out of the car and stand there, stunned, as the ground shakes from the power of ten thousand tons of steel on steel that blows my hair and clothing in all directions. After the last car crosses the intersection, I watch, dumbfounded, as the train continues silently on its journey.

"Oh, my God." I look around to see if anyone else witnessed this. "Holy— He didn't hear it. He really didn't hear it."

When we got married, Bruce and I vowed to love and forgive one another for as long as we lived. His death didn't absolve me of those promises. Here, at the last place he drew breath, I whisper, "I love you." There's nothing to forgive, for my anger is now obsolete. Bruce died a fallible human being *and* a man who loved me, loved our daughter, and loved his life.

I take a few deep breaths and look again at the farm, shrouded in mist. It was there that Bruce told me that he'd want me to move on if he died, and I told him that I couldn't live without him. It's taken me twenty-four years to learn to do both. I can move on *and* keep him alive in my heart, a ghost companion, growing old with me.

We are never-ending. No train can ever stop that.

I turn around, get back in my car, and begin my journey home.

Journal entry, March 15, 2008:

Last night I had another Bruce dream, only the ending was different than the others. I could see him in our kitchen taking something out of the oven. Usually, in previous Bruce dreams, that would be the moment when something would hold me back from reaching him. This time, I was conscious of what was happening, and I told myself to participate in the dream. I went into the kitchen and jumped on his back. He grabbed my legs and laughed.

"There you are!" he said. "I've been waiting for you!"

I kissed him and told him how much I missed him. He hugged me and said he missed me, too. I woke up feeling happy instead of sad and drained.

I changed my dream! How cool is that?

Bruce would have been forty-nine years old today. Happy birthday, babe.

ACKNOWLEDGMENTS

When I shared the first draft of this memoir with my friend, Valarie, she said, "Peeling this onion has been a lifetime project."

It most certainly has.

I will always wish that March 22, 1983, had been as ordinary as the day before it, but I am grateful to many people who have helped me capture that day and my life going forward in these pages.

My story is familiar to the readers of my former newspaper column and my blogs, *Lynn's Weigh* and *Zen Bag Lady*, and I would not have had the courage to write this book without their support and the grief and weight stories they've shared with me over the years. Their perspective changed my point of view many times, which I hope I've adequately reflected.

Many thanks to Danielle Tantone and Emily Silva Hockstra, who I met in an online memoir class. The three of us formed a writing critique group, and it was their questions, constructive criticism, and keen eye for detail that molded my initial chapters into a book. They convinced me that my story was not only worth writing but that by sharing it, I might help others in their grief.

Special thanks to my initial and beta readers. Their comments helped shape the narrative beyond what I initially imagined. They include Valarie Nordstrom, Marcia

Busdeker, Jason Bouwman, Geffen Myers, Julianne Pohl, Heather Mueller, Lisa Seidman, Barb Facile, Tracie Brennen, Kait Tonti, Joy Bauer, Marie Piantanida, Merlin Peterson and Rhonda McDowell.

Fellow writer Shauna Reid lifted me over many land mines of self-doubt. Her encouragement and her book and essays about weight and body image helped me see my own weight story in a different light. Shauna also introduced me to editor Eleanor Abraham. Thank you, Eleanor, for challenging me to rework what wasn't working, and for the countless corrections and suggestions. You can take the girl out of Minnesota, but you can't take the Minnesota colloquialisms out of the girl.

Many thanks to Allison K Williams and Dinty W. Moore, whose workshops, webinars, books, and personal guidance gave me the tools and the confidence to tell my story.

Thank you, Diane Zinna, for your Sunday Grief Writing prompts, which helped me write from a deeper understanding of my grief. Your kind and gentle spirit continues to inspire me.

I owe my life to the tough love and guidance of my therapists, "Dr. Angry," "Amy," and Julie McCune. Grief is complicated, painful, and scary, and I hope my story will encourage anyone who struggles with grief to find help through therapy. While grief never goes away, I am proof that you can learn to live with it in the same space as all the love that you think has nowhere to go.

When people ask me where I'm from, I always say Jasper, Minnesota. My roots in the Jasper community run deep, planted when all of my great-grandparents emigrated from Norway in the late-nineteenth and early-twentieth centuries. While I've not lived in Jasper for many years, I am grateful for the continued friendships of many of the people from the area including Lisa and Curt, Jeanine, Robin, Rick, Shelia, Cindy B., Cindy F., Jo and Howard, Rhonda, JK, Susan, Tina, Donna, Linda, Joyce, Dean, Randy, Carlene L., Mary S., Mary F., Tina, Barb, Brenda, Angie, Carla, Penney, Rob, Nila, Brian, Beth, Kara, Sheryl, my nieces Janel and Jeanne, and nephews Jason, Wendell, Todd, and Scott.

Thank you, also, to everyone in the Jasper and Edgerton communities who shared their memories of Bruce with our daughter Carlene when she was creating her senior project in 1999. Rereading your comments twenty years later reminded me how much Bruce was loved and missed.

A special thank you to David Mohn, without whom I would still believe that time heals.

Rodney Sherman, there's nothing I can write here that I haven't said to you a thousand times. Thank you for all of it, my friend.

Thank you to Ellen Bass for her beautiful poem *The Thing Is*, from which I titled this book.

Without Miranda Dillon from Koehler Books, I don't know when this book would have been published. Thank you for believing in my words and for catching those things that I never would have. Thank you, John Koehler, for your marketing wisdom, and Christine Kettner for your beautiful cover and interior design.

My father's love for me and support of my work were unwavering. I hope my words honor the grieving boy and man he was.

I am fortunate to love and live with an amazing partner who grounds me, supports me, and loves me just the way I am. Jim O'Hara is not afraid of or threatened by my past, and in the years we've been together, he's taught me how to stay through tough times, even though grief taught me to run away.

Always and forever, my daughters are number one in my heart. Carlene and Cassie, I love you fiercely, and that balancing act between love and my fear of loss is still a struggle. I raised you in my grief, and I know it was difficult sometimes. But despite the bad, the good has prevailed. I'm so proud of both of you and grateful that my fate has not been yours.

Printed in the USA
CPSIA information can be obtained
at www.ICGtesting.com
CBHW032311030224
3940CB00004B/14